A Commoning Heritage

The Mansbridges of Longdown

Collected and edited by Jo Ivey

Published by
Ytene Artizans
Myrtle, Main Road, East Boldre, SO42 7WU

ISBN: 978-0-9568990-0-2

Typeset by
Ytene Artizans
Myrtle, Main Road, East Boldre, SO42 7WU

Printed by
Hobbs the Printers Ltd, Totton, Hampshire SO40 3WX

FSC
www.fsc.org
MIX
Paper from
responsible sources
FSC® C020438

Photograph acknowledgements

1) Commoner Harry Burt outside his cottage in South Weirs (Christopher Tower New Forest Reference Library)

2) George Mansbridge (Joan Hayward)

3) The Mansbridge family (Mansbridge family)

4) The Mansbridge family outside Farringdon Farm thought to show Daniel as a baby in his mother's arms (Joan Hayward)

5) Jessie Mansbridge on the occasion of her 90th birthday in 1958 (Joan Hayward)

6) New Forest Gypsies beside one of their benders (Christopher Tower New Forest Reference Library)

7) Cutting hay at Acres Down, Minstead (Christopher Tower New Forest Reference Library)

8) Highland Regiment marching through Lyndhurst camp in 1914 (Christopher Tower New Forest Reference Library)

9) Indian soldiers with mules at Ashurst (Christopher Tower New Forest Reference Library)

10) Nellie Mansbridge in uniform(Mansbridge family)

11) Uncle Charlie (seated) in the Coldstream Guards (Mansbridge family)

12) Rank Flour Mills in Southampton after a bombing raid (Southampton City Archives)

13) Southampton firemen tackling fires after a night's bombing (Southampton City Archives)

14) The Homestead in 2010 (author's photograph)

15) Len as a small boy on a pony (Marion Ingram)

16) Len mounted on Rodeo (Marion Ingram)

17) Len on Black Jack (right) with Buffy (Marion Ingram)

18) Fred Norris Senior outside his shop in Beaulieu (Fred Norris).

19) Buffy Mansbridge and Jean Henvest in the Fox and Hounds in Lyndhurst (Michael Clarke)

Photographs on front cover: courtesy of the Mansbridge family.

Photograph on back cover: still image taken from video. Photographer: Jonathan Blease. © 2010 stories4change

Preface

The Mansbridges of Longdown had its origins in a telephone call from Joan Hayward (née Mansbridge) following the publication of *Keeping the Forest*[1] in 1995. Joan asked me if I would consider interviewing her father, Dan Mansbridge, who had many good stories of his life to tell.

Over the next couple of years I interviewed Dan (and sometimes his wife Ivy too) many times at their home at Shootash near Romsey. Dan's story, and that of his parents and siblings, dating back to the early part of the twentieth century - and even earlier - began to emerge.

I also got to know Len Mansbridge, Dan's nephew, quite well. Len, who has been described as the last full time commoner, lived at Ashurst, and I met him often at drifts and pony sales. I started to ask him about some of the things that Dan had told me about his family at Longdown and soon came to realise that the story that Dan had been telling me was one, not just of a single person, but of a whole family – a commoning heritage. And so I decided that I would ask Len if I could interview him too.

The work progressed slowly. I was working full time, as well as running my holding in East Boldre and taking an active part in the commoning community and the Forest. Over the next few years I collected many hours of recordings of Len, as well as making several more visits to Shootash to see Dan. Sadly Ivy had died in 1997, but Dan remained active and still delivered hay and feed. Then, in September 2001, I met Len on the East Boldre drift and told him that I must go back to see Dan about some points that weren't clear in his story. 'Oh, he died a couple of weeks back.' Len said. I was shocked and saddened by this news, but knew that his stories would be a lasting legacy of his life.

I worked on with Len and, although my life has sometimes made me set aside this important work, I always hoped to complete it during Len's lifetime. Sadly this was not to be. With the stories edited and reviewed by Len and members of his family, photographs secured, and publishing being considered, it was clear that Len's strength was failing him. He died

---

[1] Ivey, J (1995) *Keeping the Forest: The Life Story of Jack Humby, Forest Keeper.* NGK Press, Lymington, Hampshire.

on 12th February 2011 and this book is now the legacy of both Dan and Len, members of a New Forest family who lived in an age that is gone for ever.

Acknowledgements

A Commoning Heritage is the result of the work and generosity of many people who have contributed their time, their memories and their knowledge to this story of the lives of commoners in the New Forest from the early days of the twentieth century to the present day. First I must thank all those members of the Mansbridge family who have allowed me into their homes and given me the time needed to collect, edit and arrange the family's history. They have been generous with the loan of family photographs, put me right when I got things wrong and filled in gaps where the stories just didn't seem to add up.

I must also thank others who have encouraged me over the many years that it has taken to bring this book to publication, and given me background information and a new perspective. These include Richard Reeves, the librarian of the Christopher Tower Reference Library at the New Forest Centre, Graham Parkes of Waterside Heritage, Joanne Smith of Southampton City Archives, David Lambley of Longdown Estates, Mark Street and Pauline Parks of the Forestry Commission, and commoners Shirley Bell, Ann Sevier, Michael Clarke, Carole and Mike Cooper.

Finally, this book would not exist without the interest and time of Dan and Len Mansbridge. It is dedicated to them both.

Foreword by Joan Hayward and Marion Ingram

Our fathers were members of a large family that lived in the small hamlet of Longdown on the eastern edge of the New Forest. They were both brought up in hard times but, being country folk, they overcame any problems that arose. We were both brought up in the locality, too, and have long loved the many places and people that they talk about.

Dan Mansbridge

My dad – what can I say? He loved to communicate with people and was a good and trusted person, although he would be the first to say that he was not perfect in all he said and did!

He was a person who loved nature and a natural way of living that - in his younger days - would include a bit of poaching to help support his family. He found a thrill in setting a hen on a batch of eggs for hatching, and he always made sure his farm animals were fed and bedded down for the night in winter.

He was also concerned to make his customers happy on his round in Southampton where he traded with his farm produce: milk, vegetables, rabbits, chickens and eggs.

And he always had respect for the Gypsy folk who lived in the Forest and learnt a lot from them. If ever he had an animal sick or in trouble, Dad knew he could trust them to help.

He had a wonderful mother who gave him a good start in life by her hard working, gentle, Christian faith, which Dad followed as best he could. I am sure her influence was of great importance to the way he enjoyed his natural surroundings.

Joan Hayward
April 2011

Len Mansbridge

I guess you could say Dad had an apprenticeship to life from a very early age, and he came to appreciate it as his life unfolded. When I was a child at Hythe my sister, Sheila, and I spent many happy hours playing in the fields (our brother, Lenny, was still a baby at that time), oblivious of the hard life that my parents were living.

We moved to Ashurst and Dad really did start on the bottom rung of the ladder; but over the years he built up his holding to a successful business. To do this, holidays were a definite no go, except for days out at market or a horse sale – never down to the beach! As we children got older and learned to ride, I think it gave him great pleasure to take a few hours off to go to the odd show, point-to-point and to the races.

He loved the Forest and all it stood for, which led him to get involved in all the local organisations of the Forest. There were certain plants in the Forest I think he felt personally responsible for: - the royal fern, the wild violets and the wild gladioli. After winter, particularly if it had been a hard one, he'd would go and check to see if they had survived.

Len was the last of a long line of Mansbridges of his generation who cared deeply for the Forest on his doorstep.

Marion Ingram
April 2011

Introduction: New Forest Commoners

The history of the New Forest is the history of its commoners. This form of agriculture, which was once widespread across much of Britain and Europe, has survived in the New Forest largely because it became a royal forest in the eleventh century. William the Conqueror's hunting grounds were controlled by Forest Law, which prohibited the clearance of land for agriculture and also restricted the use of the open common land in order to protect the deer – not only as a sport for the king and his gentry - but also as a valuable source of food for the royal table.

At that time the use of common land to support small scale agriculture was widespread in many parts of England. As agricultural techniques improved much common land was enclosed and the rights over it were extinguished. The New Forest has survived as an area of open heathland grazed by free ranging animals largely as a result of the protection afforded to it by forest law.

The Register of Claims published in 1854[1] describes 1200 claims to common rights in the New Forest, of which 571 were 'large holders' (over 30 acres) and the remainder were 'small holders'. References to the commoner's way of life at the time appear to show that families lived well on their smallholdings mainly as a result of the additional benefit of the Forest grazing for their stock. Elsewhere the "turning out" belonging to the "small places" was described as being "as valuable as the places themselves pretty near."[2]

Although New Forest cottagers were generally not self sufficient on their land, relying on labouring and small scale trade for a steady income, Briscoe Eyre points out that the profits of the family holding compared

---

[1] W. Esdaile analysed the 1854 Register of Claims
[2] Briscoe Eyre, G E (1883) *The New Forest: Its Common Rights and Cottage Stock Keepers*, J C Short, Lyndhurst , p32.

favourably to those of a farm about three times its size, and twice its rent, as a result of the benefits gained through the exercise of common rights. His description of the Forest at the time of his report describes the woods and heaths, with low-lying, fertile lawns and 'Here and there, a brown hamlet on high ground, or a stray cottage with its little plot and orchard, nestling in some sheltered hollow or skirting the roadside'. Well established holdings included a garden and orchard, with buildings including a 'cottage, cowpen and pigstye'.[3]

Commoner Harry Burt outside his cottage in South Weirs

During the nineteenth century the quiet of the Forest began to be eroded when the London to Southampton railway was extended into south-west Hampshire and into Dorset in 1847. The line ran right through the heart of the New Forest and allowed an influx of new residents to the area. This '"new gentry" flocking into the district, many of them to old lodges

---

[3] Briscoe Eyre, *ibid,* p50.

and "service cottages" put on the estate market perhaps by the Office of Woods as "superior gentlemen's residences in beautiful and romantic surroundings."[4] And gradually, the improvement of the road network in the area allowed the opening up of the Forest to more residential development and led to the growth of the population across the Forest.

Longdown

The parish of Colbury lies at the north eastern edge of the Forest, close to Southampton Water. At the turn of the twentieth century the parish included Longdown, an area of land between the open Forest in the west, and Southampton Water in the east, that was part of the Barker Mills estate. The Longdown Road runs north-south, parallel with Southampton Water, meeting the road from Lyndhurst to Southampton at its northern end and the road from Marchwood to the open Forest in the south. The roads and branching network of tracks are dotted with small holdings which, at the beginning of the twentieth century, were home to more than 50 families, the majority of whom were estate tenants who lived by farming and work in the woods around them.

At that time Marianne Vaudrey Barker-Mill ran the estate with a benign, if sometimes authoritarian, hand. She considered herself to be the 'benefactoress of the estate' and had already contributed to the building of Colbury Church (1871). After World War I, she built a village hall at Colbury which is dedicated to the memory of her son, and other men from the estate who were killed in the war.[5] It is reported by some of the estate's present tenants that she insisted that all properties on the estate were fully occupied. Thus, if a husband or wife died, tenants were expected to re-marry within six months, or risk losing their home.

---

[4] Kenchington, F E (1944). *The Commoners' New Forest.* Hutchinson, London.p112. Although David Stagg points out the New Forest Act of 1877 prevented the Forestry Commission from selling off its holdings in the New Forest, and that this bar remained until 1981.

[5] *The Barker-Mill Story: A Hampshire family since the 16th century.* Tessa Lecomber, Trustees of the Barker-Mill Family, 2000.

The 1901 Census of Population records that, of the 56 families then living there, half the heads of household, and over half (51) of all recorded workers were employed in agriculture. A further third (30) of workers were employed in other kinds of work (building, general labour, etc), 11 were domestic workers (cook, gardener, servant) and 6 were described as wood dealers or woodsmen.

During the nineteenth and well into the twentieth century the great majority of the cottagers relied on the Forest for at least part of their living. Every morning one or two house cows would be sent out of each cottage gate to walk up the lane and graze the Forest until they returned to be milked and bedded down for the night in the evening. A typical holding had enough land for a vegetable plot and chickens, and most would kill at least two pigs a year: one for the rent and one for the family to eat. However, Longdown was not isolated. Southampton was only 5 miles away to the east, the railway at Lyndhurst Road station was two miles by road to the north west (or one mile across the Forest). The families who lived in the area travelled away to work and trade on a regular basis.

The Mansbridge family

The Mansbridge family, whose story is told in this book, is known to have lived in Longdown since at least the early part of the 19th century. Charles Mansbridge was born in Twiggs Lane in 1820 and married Mary Luke, also of Twiggs Lane, in 1844. They had seven children of whom George, father of Dan and grandfather of Leonard, was born in 1855.

George's mother died in 1862 when he was 8 years old and when he was nine, at the time of the 1871 census, George was living alone with his father. His older sisters had all married, and his brothers, Michael (18) and Jacob (12) were living with his married sister, Sarah (known as Sally) and her husband James Osman.

During the nineteenth century much local employment was based in the woods of the Barker Mill's estate in the area around Marchwood. In the censuses of the period, a number of men are recorded with the occupation of 'wood dealer', 'wood cutter', 'woodsman', while some women are also recorded as being 'wood tier', 'bark cutter', and so on.

From the time of the 1871 census, George was recorded as being a 'labourer in the woods', alongside his father. Dan's recollection from the stories he had been told about his father's youth was that, during the winter he worked in the woods around Longdown, coppicing the trees for sticks, poles and faggots which he sold in Southampton. In the summer he, and a number of other young men from the area, would travel to farms across the south, seeking casual agricultural work.

Charles Mansbridge died in 1876, and by 1881 George was living with his sister, Sally, her husband James Osman, and James' elderly mother in Staplewood Lane (probably at Dumpers Farm, which is where Sally and James were living in 1901). His aunt and her husband did not have any children of their own and George and Jacob were amongst four young men living there as 'farm labourers'.

George Mansbridge

In 1882 George married Louisa Kate Harvey. Kate was born in Ampfield, in North Hampshire, in 1859. By the time of the 1871 Census, she was recorded as the daughter of the landlord of the Bold Forester pub in Beaulieu Road, where her father also farmed 21 acres. The 1881 census also found her there.

Following their marriage, George and Kate Mansbridge lived at Staplewood Farm on Staplewood Lane, where they had three children. Rebecca Kate was the first, born in 1883, but she only lived 9 months. Her brother, Edwin George (always known as Ted), was born in 1885, and lived on to be 88 years old. A second son, Mark, was born in 1887 but only lived five years.

It was a tragic family. Louisa fell ill when her two boys were small and a young local woman, Jessie Green, came in to help keep house and look after the children. Louisa died in 1891, but Jessie stayed on to keep house for the family.

Jessie Green was born in a cottage called Farringdon in Twiggs Lane End in 1868, which was a holding of 22 acres. Jessie had 3 older brothers and a sister, and she was followed by 5 younger siblings. At 13 she had gone into the service of a family in Shirley, Southampton. However, when her mother died in 1882, she came home to take care of her younger brothers and sisters.

Two years later her father died in an accident, leaving Jessie to bring up her younger brothers and sisters. She worked on the holding and took on the family's grocery round, carrying vegetables and poultry into Southampton twice a week. Her older brother, James, was not interested in the holding, leaving much of the work to Jessie. When he surrendered the tenancy in 1891, George Mansbridge took it on. The following year they were married, and started their own family. They had nine children, eight of whom survived into adulthood, and old age. Only little Winifred, who contracted tetanus at the age of ten, died as a child.

Dan Mansbridge: 1906 to 2001

A Forest upbringing

Dan was George and Jessie's eighth child, born in 1906. His memories of his childhood and the people who lived around him in Longdown offer a fascinating account of a way of life long since passed into history. Not only did the family continue to work the land and raise livestock at Farringdon. They also expanded the grocery round that Jessie's family had started, carrying vegetables, poultry and later, fresh milk, into Southampton.

Dan was a child when the First World War took two of his older brothers and one of his sisters off to Europe. He witnessed the build up of troops in the Lyndhurst area, and watched their manoeuvres, as they prepared to embark for France. He also saw the effects that life in the trenches would have on his brother, who told him some of the horrors that he experienced.

He married Ivy May Smith in 1930. She lived in one of the cottages in Longdown, and they had known each other all their lives. When she was young her father kept a small holding and hired out a cart. But her family had the tenancy of the Bold Forester and, when she was older, her father took it over from his father.

From the viewpoint of the western fringes of the city, he witnessed the devastating bombing of the city of Southampton in the Second World War. This frequently extended into the Forest where numerous airfields were established, and troops and armaments awaited D-Day away from the main population centres. The farm where he and his young family were living at the start of the war was badly damaged in a bombing raid, and they had to move back to his parents' home at Farringdon. He took over the tenancy from his father in 1942 and continued the grocery round throughout the bombardment. On his regular trips to the city he witnessed the after effects of nights of bombing on the city's population.

In 1951 Dan gave up the tenancy of Farringdon. By that time, the grocery round had become redundant, as improved transport links brought food into Southampton from far afield. Dan's business was moving into different areas of trade and, with a growing family to provide for, he felt he had outgrown the rented small holding that he had been born in, and moved out of the Forest to become the owner occupier of a farm at Shootash, near Romsey.

The recordings on which the following chapters are based were made in 1996 and '97, when Dan was 90 and his wife, Ivy, was 86. These have been edited and combined in places with descriptions taken from a short text that Dan wrote about himself, called 'A little of my life'. At the time of the recordings, they lived in their farmhouse at Romsey, and Dan still went out regularly with his son to deliver hay and feedstuffs to surrounding farms.

My father George Mansbridge had been married before he married my mother. His first wife died early leaving three children: 2 boys and a girl. The girl died when she was about 6 months old and one of the boys died of asthma at 5 years of age. The other lived to be 92 years of age. While my father's first wife was ill, my mother nursed her. My mother, whose name was Jessie Green, looked after the children until a few years later they were married. Then my father, who had been living at Arters Lawn, moved over to live with my mother at Farringdon Farm.

We were a very close family in every way. Both my parents were devoted Christians. We had our little Wesleyan chapel at Longdown which we, when we were children, attended 3 times a day on Sundays. We always had Bible readings and prayers, no matter how busy my parents were, every day, morning and evening. They helped to support and keep our little Chapel going for years, Mother being Sunday School Superintendent for 75 years. Father was chapel keeper for about 30 years.

My parents were very hard working. Not much of this world's goods, but they brought us up to be a very happy family. People today have no idea how, in the early part of this century, people brought up their family on a small holding. My parents had nine children which they fed and clothed all very well. We always had plenty to eat. They done so much planning for the future in all sorts of ways, making lots of jam and pickles, storing lots of fruit, especially lots of apples.

I suppose, being such a close family those first twenty odd years were perhaps the happiest of my life. As children, we didn't have anything, but we were happy. Happy – all of us – together. We always had things – I can't remember very much about birthdays - but Christmas always had something, didn't know what, never knew what, but we always had something.

From a very early time of my life I liked work and still do today. I think that work should be part of life's pleasure. My parents, who must have been very contented, taught us this very important, can I say, virtue: contentment, which I believe is far more precious than all the money this world can give. I do not mean we should sit back and let the world go by, but not be always worrying about money. I do not want to boast because I have always tried to do my work for the best reward.

The Mansbridge family. Left to right: Dorothy, George, Rose, Winifred, Nellie, Jessie, Daniel

Life seemed so steady and purposeful in those days. We had very hard times in the 1920's and 1930's, with the country in deep financial trouble, much harder than in recent years – with so many unemployed with very little benefit. I think my parents left such a wonderful impression on us children through those hard times. Having said all that, I am sure that hardship makes for a better prospect for young people to live in later life. I myself learnt more about good husbandry from my father and others of his age than all the books about this subject -- and my father did not have much of what we call today education. He left school at 8 years of age and my mother at 10, yet they were very good in business and brought up a family of 9 on a small Forest holding of 28 acres.

My father worked in the woods, cutting – most of his life: all through the winter, anyway. He worked on the Manor in the woods, cutting what we called underwood. The wood was clean then – there wasn't any rubbish, because, you see, everything was used right down to all the bushes: all the thorns, all the crab apples – there were lots of crab apples in there. That was all cut up and tied up into little bundles for the baker. They used to cut the underwood every 8 to 10 years. If they could get the Manor to leave them a bit longer they would, because you got bigger poles for the people in the town for gardens, with their roses.

And then in the summer, as a young man, he and perhaps half a dozen or eight of them would go down, just into Sussex, and around there helping on the farm, you know hoeing ... HOEING wheat! By hand! I think different than any of the people do today, and get into trouble over it. Because I still say that we could have done without all this fertiliser and weed killers if we kept up with hand hoeing. You can have machinery to go through and loosen the ground up but there's nothing like the hoe that lets the air into the ground.

And that again, he told me that on the farm where they used to go a lot: the biggish estates somewhere down there, they wouldn't even let you cut the wheat with a scythe. You had to cut it with a hook. I've cut lots with a hook, you know. Me and my brother used to cut with one: with a scythe you tend to lose a few, you see. My father with a hook: I've never seen anyone cut the way he could. It was what he'd learned as a child. Didn't matter whether it was cutting bracken, or anything. And he could sharpen hooks! Cor! Or an axe, anything of that: like a razor. And, of course, when he was away and we had a bit of cutting, whether it was bracken or whatever it was, we used to try to go and get his hook. And as soon he come – or whenever he went to use the hook,

'Who's been using my hook?' He knew the moment, you see, but he wasn't really angry.

All round the Forest: commoners – lots of them – I could count up only what I knew round, did get – actually get – their living off that little bit of a holding and turning to the Forest. People have said, I've heard it said, how my father and others were pretty hard men. They had to be hard men to make a living!

Farringdon was right on down the bottom of the rough old forest track. If you go from Colbury, down before you get to the Bold Forester, there's a lane turns right out to the open forest. There's a little holding there, that they call Foxhills. Down a bit of a lane and across a field to get to that. And then there was another cottage, what they called Farringdon Cottage. That was across another 2 or 3 fields.

But all that way led off the road: the only way, really, in for us was down by the school at Longdown and right to the far end to Farringdon Farm. That was always our way in and out. And the Gypsies were right on our border: on the forest.

People with horses and carts using the Forest would use the track quite a bit. And there was great big holes and ruts. In fact the only thing to fill them up was the Gypsies with their shavings off the pegs they were making. Yes it was. They'd come and fill these holes with all their shavings. It was full of great big holes where we used it so many years.

Years afterwards, the first motor vehicle we got, we had to do something about it. Before that the Forestry wouldn't let you have the gravel, or anything to do anything, but I did get permissions then, and I pecked, 2 or 3 hundred yards of gravel in my spare time, from the Forest. I had a permission to, as long as it was put on the Forest.

The house and land was all rented off the Barker Mill Estate. And I've no complaints about the old people, Barker Mill. They were very good, very good you know, to everyone really. I remember one time, before I took anything on or anything. I can't remember how many years ago: it was in the depression and I suppose things had really got bad and people couldn't get the rent up together. And she came round, the old lady – and she very seldom went out of her big house that she had up at Colbury. She and her daughter went round to most of the people and said 'Look, don't worry about the rent this time'.

The Mansbridge family outside Farringdon Farm (thought to show Daniel as a baby in his mother's arms and brother Ted in the foreground)

The cottage had three rooms downstairs and three up. There had been only 4 rooms and, I suppose, when all the children come along, my father had 2 rooms put on. He got permission from the estate to have 2 rooms on. And do you know how much it cost him to put those two – and it's 2 really good rooms, except they're a bit sloped up. They're brick – all brick and with thatch. How much do you think they charged him to put 2 rooms up? Twenty-two pounds!

We were usually up about half past seven, children and all, because we had to get ready and go to school. Father was already up. He was always up early, I don't know really what time. We had a place down in the field where we kept pigs and kept them on for pork, and that paid the rent. We had a copper in the copper house, and he always used to go down and light that, get it going before he had his breakfast. Then, everything else, cattle and all that. I suppose before we came along, he used to do it all, and we carried on with it afterwards. We always used to go down and muck out before breakfast. You know, the main, everything, cleaning up ready for milking. Then later on in the day when you turned them out, you'd clean out.

My eldest sister stayed home to look after us younger children while my father and mother went to Southampton. She kept me home until I was 6, so leaving school at 12 ½, I had six years at school. I think there was seventy-eight to eighty at school at Longdown and, when the First World War came, they couldn't get teachers: they had gone to the war – nursing and all that. The old governess that was there had seven classes - seven classes! She done the whole lot. She was only a little bit of a thing. Mind you, she did rule the roost sort of thing. She never had any trouble there.

Jessie Green: mother, trader and friend of the Gypsies

Dan's memories of his mother were full of praise and admiration for this woman who brought up her own brothers after her mother's death, and then went to help bring up those of her neighbour when their mother fell ill. She married the children's widowed father and brought up 10 children in the little farmhouse. At the same time she ran a poultry business, delivering eggs and dressed chickens into Southampton two days a week for many years. Above all, though, Dan remembers her for her love of the little chapel at Longdown, and the local Gypsies.

My mother had two brothers older then her and one sister and then there was one brother and three sisters younger. She went out to service, I think when she was about 13, something like that. Then her mother died after giving birth to her last sister so she came home and helped with her two older brothers to run the place. She was only about fifteen when she came home, and she brought up the others, the younger sisters and brother.

It wasn't long after that her father died. He was killed by a road accident. They were racing, which they used to with horses. I've seen them on the road there. They were all coming over Redbridge, the Old Causeway, and he had an accident, and he never recovered. He didn't live very long.

She had to look after everything, and struggled on for a long time. You think of it at 15: coming home, taking charge! I suppose they already had a little round in Southampton, of some sort, and after a while she took that on.

Later on, when she probably got nearly twenty – something of that – my father, who was married, lived over on Arters Lawn, and his wife was very ill. So my mother went and nursed her. They had three children then, two boys and girl. The girl only lived about a couple of months I think[6]. So that left two boys and she was going over, until their mother died and then I suppose it wasn't so long before she decided she would marry my father.

Her brother – the oldest brother – wasn't very helpful to her, taking advantage of what little was coming in from the farm. He kept the tenancy at Farringdon on for a bit, but he couldn't keep the rent up and all that. He was a bit of a waster and so – I don't remember what went on – but, anyway, they took my father on as a tenant as he was already on the estate.

One of the two boys died when he was about six. He suffered with asthma, terrible! That left one of my father's and we thought of him more than a brother to us. In all, there was nine of us and then there was ten, if you follow me.

My mother brought us all up. How she got round to it, I just don't understand: I mean I know what work is. Never ever once did I hear her complain about anything! Financially or anything. And anyone who needed help or anything she would go and do it and think nothing of it. And she brought us all up. Before that, she did all sorts of things for everybody.

The more I think about it: she looked after the poultry, made the butter. We'd have 3 or 4 hundred hens running all free range. They'd go anywhere to lay their eggs: in the Forest and all. They were mostly Rhode Island crosses. She used to rear a lot of chicks. April, May time, she used to hatch perhaps three or four hundred or something of that, under hens. We had a big part of the barn, when it come round to hatching time and she'd have a row of proper nest boxes, the big long nest boxes and, we'd hatch out all the chickens. Sometime we'd have 3, 4 or 5 hundred, little chicks! She used to try to hatch them mostly together – less work – and they'd all be

---

[6] Dan is mistaken here. The sister, Rebecca Kate, had died as a baby in 1883, long before Jessie came to help nurse her mother, Louisa Kate Mansbridge.

coming along together. But then she used to always be having a few extra and they'd go right on into the end of the year.

All the cockerels she used to kill, pluck and dress: all went with the living. My father used to do quite a bit of the milking but, if he was doing other things, Mother and any of the children would help milk the cows We boys would take turns. We only had, perhaps we'd keep 12 or 14 cows, something of that.

We used to help with the plucking, but no-one ever could pluck a chicken as quick as her. After I'd killed it, she'd pluck it because she could do it faster than I could. I remember once, we'd got to the top gate and she usually had them all down on a list: I don't know, a dozen, fifteen, anything like, when they were available. And we'd get up to the top gate and she'd say 'Oh, I haven't got so and so……. I haven't got enough chickens! I've got to get one for someone…..' We'd go back down and she'd get the one she wanted and I used to kill 'em. She'd pluck it and dress it in 10 minutes!

My mother paid a penny a week, I think, to go to school, when she could afford it. Yet she could talk to anyone better than ever I could. She could meet anyone. We had all sorts of people as customers, like vets and two or three captains of ships, their children used to come out to our place at Farringdon. It was all pretty rough, but they used to come out and enjoy coming out.

She used to run the Sunday School up at the chapel, and she always got round and have a Christmas tree for the children, and a tea. There was a lot of children in Longdown and around about at that time. And then within 2 or 3 days she'd have another one for the Gypsies and know all the children. And the Gypsies were thought of -- she'd find something for every one of them.

Her main love was the Gypsies. She'd do anything, anything for them. If any of them was ill she'd go straight away up and see them. Anytime they wanted – anything. If they wanted letters written, anything of that, they would come down to us. I never wrote any letters, but my sister did.

I remember once, I couldn't have been more then seven; I hadn't been going to school all that time. Me and two of my sisters came home from school. Must of been November, December time because it was dark, pouring with rain, that night. And we arrived, both thinking to ourselves, pleased to get home. We knew when we got to the back door the Gypsies had been around because in the smoke and all that you could almost smell them. We walked in and Mother had six or seven or eight of them sat all round the fire, drying them out. And we weren't very pleased at that. We wanted our tea! I never said anything about it to anyone. Only 'til about a couple or three months ago I was in with my sister and we were talking about it and she said, 'Do you remember the Gypsies sat round the fire?' and I said, 'Look, I never said anything to anyone about it because I wanted to make sure that it was so.' And it was so.

Jessie Mansbridge on the occasion of her 90th birthday in 1958

I don't know whether she had them in any other time, but they were always round the back door. They were always coming down for milk. They knew the time when we were separating, and the milk was all warm coming out. They'd all come in there. Sometimes, there was a little queue outside, a crowd of them, all with their bottles. Mother would fill the bottles up and they'd have a drink and fill them up again, and all that sort of thing.

There's a story about the Gypsies' memories of my mother after all the years. Until about 5, 6, 7 years ago, I used to sell a lot down round Hardley, Holbury and round that area and Beaulieu. I used to go to a place down in the bottom, round the back of Lime Kiln Lane. There's a pub down in the bottom: The Old Mill, up through a little bit of track. There's a Mr Goodridge lived there. I got to know him very well because they had horses up in there. Well I hadn't been going there quite so much for a while and I went in just to see how he was. I was down the bottom and I thought, that looks like one of the Gypsies, though I couldn't have sworn by it. A lot of them had horses there with Goodridge. After I was gone, this - Cooper his name was - he said, 'Was that Dan Mansbridge down there?' Goodridge said, 'Yes. Do you know him then?' Cooper said, 'When I was a boy, 45 or 50 years ago I knew him very well. I'll tell you one thing, I knew his mother and she was the best lady in the world!'

That was saying something: it all came out. Goodridge told me this. They all did: they thought mother was a little queen like. Most of the men and women, boys and girls they all thought it.

The Gypsies of Longdown

The Gypsies who lived at Longdown were part of the wider New Forest Gypsy population which moved between haunts in the Forest and further afield in Kent and Sussex, following the seasonal agricultural tasks. Dan grew up amongst them, learnt to respect them and value their knowledge. He might even have joined them if they would have had him.

He called them the police of the Forest: they knew what was going on across the open wastes and, though they were often blamed for things gone missing or trouble started, his only criticism of them was their liking for a few beers of a Saturday evening which often led to high spirits and sometimes quarrels between them.

The worst thing that ever happened, Dan thought, was the advent of the 'compounds' to which local Gypsy families were confined in the 1920's. Families registered there were kept track of by the Keepers, their nomadic lifestyle was severely restricted, and the conditions in the compounds were unhealthy. The compounds were the first stage in the destruction of the Gypsy way of life in the New Forest which ended in the 1960's, when the compounds were cleared and the remaining families were settled into housing.

The Gypsies we knew at first were the real Gypsies. They were mostly local: if they went away they, came back to the same haunt – almost always. We got to know them very well. Then, when the war came along, they left them alone they didn't move them on. A lot of them went in the army, so mostly through the war the rest stayed put. They used to go away for perhaps a week to earn a bit of money during the war like, if they could, hoeing or anything, but not quite the same as before or after the war.

New Forest Gypsies beside one of their benders

They used to come down and get my sister to write a letter for them. They hadn't been to school very much, not at that time. I remember there was one used to come down, he lived on his own: Puffer Whale (he was always puffing: he was a smoker) He got my sister to write this letter. He was sending a big plum cake to his son for Christmas. When he got to the end he said, 'Put a few kisses!' My sister filled up the pages with kisses to his son.

A lot of the men had gone to the war, and the children went to school. I went to school with quite a few of them. I sat next to one of them for a long time. He turned out quite a nice chap. He got to be the foreman on the telephone. They were marvellous: children and all! All the children, I mean, they were our friends. Even my sisters and that – all of us – played with them. I used to gamble with them a bit; I only thought of that the other day. I used to play pitch and toss. They were good at it, well of course, you bet whatever you had: a penny or whatever. The one who got nearest to the mark, he had the first toss. Throw them up, either head or tails, whichever, that was his. It was only fun.

They were wonderful. I could have went and lived with them quite easily, but they wouldn't have accepted me. Just the same we say about the Gypsies: the girls, they were pretty. They didn't wear any make up or anything. They were pretty! I nearly fell for one. Her brother said to me one day, he said, 'Do you know, it's no good for you to go on with Harriet' (I believe her name was). He said 'They won't never accept you'. No they wouldn't. I wasn't good enough for them, you see.

Our next door neighbour was a Bull, and he married a Doe. She was a Gypsy and they wouldn't accept him. After they got married, they had a tent just over in this Mr. Bull's field. They stayed there for quite a long time and then they moved down to Sandy Hill just above Applemore. They got a house there. There's one or two of the descendants from them now.

We never ever had any trouble with them. The only time they were a bit rowdy was when they'd been down to the Bold Forester. We knew Saturday night, we'd hear them start quarrelling a bit. They would go down to the pub and you would hear them coming back. You could hear them all the way back up. The dogs barking and that they would get up to the tents. I've known my father go up and say, 'What's the matter here then? Be quiet'. That would be the end of it.

We used to go up and listen to what was going on in the dark. Me and my brother Charlie were up there one night. This Bert Doe, you could tell he was a little bit quarrelsome coming up through the Forest. We pushed on to get up out in our field, so we could see what happened. 'Well', he said, 'I'll fight any man there is in Longdown tonight. I don't care if it be me brother or me brother-in-law or who it is. I'll fight any man there is in Longdown tonight. Now come on.' he said. It was the drop of drink that did it.

This Bert Doe: I'll tell you a little bit about him. Now he was in three wars. He went to the Boer War. In the First War, I believe, he got up to a sergeant, and then in the Second World War he was up Winchester, training.

Then there was another old one, Matty Jeff. He was only a little man. He could make a bee pot that would hold water. I've had a go trying to make them. Even my mother, she couldn't make them, but she used to make baskets and that. In the summer, he always used to have a little tent and he used to have his feet right outside the tent. And me and my brother used to go up – if he was there, like – and get a holly bush and tickle his feet – and run. Of course, he never knew who it was, because we were gone. That was me and my brother, Charlie.

All in all, the Gypsies as we knew them, if we wanted anything done, we'd lost or missed a cow or anything, we'd only have to go up to them. All the menfolk would turn out and walk over in the Forest where they thought it might have got in a bog or anything. Anywhere there was forest fires and the gorse blackstems[7] they'd clear them up. Really they used to keep the Forest clean

There was times when the camp was empty if they went out fruit picking or hoeing or anything. Perhaps you'd have a fortnight, three weeks when it would be clear. When they went, I don't think they all went the same way, but they all seemed to separate and go out and come back within about a fortnight or 3 weeks. They mostly came back to one of the haunts there close. When they went you felt you'd lost something.

---

[7] Blackstem is the burnt branches of gorse left after controlled burning of the heath. It is still used as kindling and for burning in domestic fires.

They were good at hoeing, strawberry picking, hop picking. Everybody said how good they were. They say they grew their nails a bit longer before they went strawberry picking because they had to pick the stem off with the strawberry. From what I remember, first of all, they'd go away – usually about a fortnight they were gone – along in April: that was for hoeing the strawberries, over at Swanwick and round that area. By the time they'd finished hoeing them, they'd straw them down. Then they might come back for a week or fortnight to see whether they were ripening. As soon as they were ripening, they'd go for another fortnight or 3 weeks, however long the season lasted. Between whiles they'd go perhaps up to Alton or anywhere round up that way where they used to grow hops. They'd go and hoe them and help put the sticks up and then they'd go hop picking. They used to do very well at hop picking; I think they used to build up a bit of capital sort of thing. We never had any trouble with them paying for anything, milk or anything else. It was perhaps only halfpennies or pennies but we never had any trouble.

During the winter, when they were there mostly, there were I suppose 10, a dozen, 14 families – maybe somewhere between – when they were all there, because they all went and come. There were Does, Williams, Wells, Sherwoods – quite a lot of them. When they made their tents or benders, if they had plenty of time to put them up, they done it pretty thoroughly. They bent one pole over and then they had the lew in the middle and then there'd be one perhaps going out the other way and one that way. They'd have up to 3 compartments, as the family grew.

Some, because they were there longer, we got to know better than others. All of them were very, very good. I can't remember all the slang words they had for all the different things. Marvellous! If anyone only knew the words they used now. I knew them all, or a lot of them. I was trying the other day to get them right. I knew they called we Gorgies.

They'd go making pegs, things like that, all through the winter. Where they stripped off the stakes for the pegs, they'd build up great big heaps of shavings. It wasn't much good to burn because it was all green. The wood didn't cost them anything off the forest.

They were really marvellous. They'd go and get hazel or willow -- clean sticks, no knots or anything - to make the pegs. First of all they'd chop them off, measure out with one: chop him off like that to make two pegs. And they'd pass him on to the next one and he'd strip them off, all according to how many there was round, until they got round to making the pegs.

Then they would make baskets or bee pots. Whatever it was it all came from the land. Some people tried later on to make them with straw, it wasn't like that grass that grows on the bogs. They used to go out and gather that, sit down and get a long bramble and take all the prickles off and peel it, hang it up to dry. You could pull that as tight as you liked almost. Thread it through and through.

Their knives were like razors. By the time they got right round, the last one would be putting the tin round and the little nail to hold him then cut them off in two: one stroke and they were cut off. We used to save all our cocoa tins and that sort of thing for them. They used to make thousands of pegs. It was quite a performance: I've sat round with them when they've been doing it, and tried to do it. And of course, they'd pull me leg about it: 'I've never seen one like that!' I never got round to it; I've never done one.

They used to take them into Southampton. Apart from going round the houses and selling local, any extras they had they would take them into a place in Bevois Valley in Southampton. I've known one old lady, we called her Pretty Gal – I don't know why we called her that: I suppose she was pretty. She'd go in with a pram load twice in a day (she'd get away very early in the morning). She would walk in and walk out: pushing the pram.

My father employed quite a few of them at times. Any time that he wanted anything done he'd go up if they were around - potato digging, hoeing anything there was going. We used to employ them quite a lot. They were very good at it. They never used to want to be too regular: a fortnight and that was it. Mostly, the winter, that was when they were there, moving from one haunt to the other every 24 hours.

We always used to cut the bracken out in the Forest, every little stalk was cut. We had our patch: you had your own patch of bracken: fern, we called it. This particular day we'd employed two of the Gypsies, to cut the bracken and get so many of what we called pooks, that you pick up with a fork, so many to the load. They didn't try to do you, if you wanted 40 pooks, you'd have 40 pooks, and they would be all a fair weight and size.

This particular day, it was just the other side of the railway. I had one horse and cart. I was only a boy: I had to follow Father. We got out there and we got two loads in the morning. When we went back in the afternoon to get two more loads they didn't have any cut. There was two of them there, Eanus Sherwood and Silas - two brothers.

Father said, 'What happened then, Eanus? You haven't got anything cut today.'

He said, 'Well, Mr Mansbridge, Silas got the old complaint come on.' Agew they called it. He said 'We haven't done much.'

Silas was sort of keeping out the way, so Father said, 'What's the matter with him now?' Eanus said, 'Well, I'll tell you, Mr Mansbridge. We was feeling a bit dry and we've been over the pub and had a pint a piece.'

Father said, 'Silas has had more than a pint.' He said, 'Well it's no good telling a lie about it, Mr Mansbridge, we had 2 pints each!'

Another thing, this Eanus Sherwood, he had a boy, Billy. I suppose we'd been out in the field -- I could show you the spot in the field now where we were walking along. They'd been out potato digging. Billy was strutting behind my father, in a way boys do.

Eanus, his father, looked round and said, 'Billy don't be brazen, walk along behind Mr Mansbridge as you ought to and don't be brazen.'

After a bit Billy said, 'I didn't mean anything Dad, but now I'm going to tell Mr Mansbridge what you done. When you were out in the field yesterday, you picked out 2 of the biggest taters you could find and took them home for your tea!' Father had always said to them, if you want a potato or anything, pick one up.

Then, in 1926 I believe, they put them in compounds and that was really the beginning of the trouble. Then you got no-goods from the towns or anywhere come in, scrap merchants and that sort of thing. I knew some of them. Down there it was a way out for them. They could come and live rent free. When they done that, it begin to be the end of the Gypsies as we knew them. They married into one of two of the families and it all began to break up.

In those compounds, there was nothing: no toilets. Their water they had to find from another source. They always had a spring somewhere. They'd dig out a spring and they'd go to that spring. All in all, they were all on top of each other. Instead of 7 or 8 families, you might have 30 perhaps. These other people putting up shacks and all that, not the old way of their living, the tents and their benders was gone.

After they were put in the compound, of course I was on the vegetable round, I used to take the van up on Saturday afternoon and sell quite a lot. It was easy because they all came to you; you didn't have to go to them. Some of them, the older ones they didn't change so much, it was he younger ones. You can understand they were being brought up differently. After I took over the place, I had several young ones like, then they came of age and had to go to the war.

I had one quite a while, he used to help me with the milking; he was a good milker and everything. Don't know whether he's passed on or not, I ought to have kept in touch with him. He had to stay there because he was exempt you see, but he was a good workman: ploughing, doing anything. I had another one that I knew very well. He came and worked for me quite a while, off and on. He'd only want about fortnight or three weeks and then that was enough, he'd want a change.

He used to come Saturday mornings at that time. One Friday afternoon he said, 'Can you let me have some money for the week?' I said, 'Yes, that's alright, Albert, but I shan't see you tomorrow, shall I?' 'What do you mean,' he said, 'You won't see me tomorrow!' I said, 'You know you won't come in tomorrow.' And he didn't. Then I suppose he had somebody else to go to on the Monday.

I wasn't too particular like. I didn't have too much on. He never paid me back for that half a day! After we moved up here he used to come, and he'd go round collecting blackberries. I used to say, 'When are you going to come and do that half a day for us then, Albert?' 'I'll be round one day,' he said. After a while I said, 'You keeps on saying you're going to do half a day.' He said, 'Well I've been working it out. You go back all that time and with today's prices, it isn't hardly worth coming is it?' I think that was the last time I seen him. All part of life really, but now I don't know. We'd come home at night, the Gypsies would look out the tent and we just have a word or a joke over something or other.

It makes me really cross. Leonard says the same as I do: they never ought to have taken them out of their haunts. I was talking to Jack[8] and he said, really they were a police to the Forest. I'm not saying that they didn't do the same as the Commoners all done. It's no good saying they didn't. I knew enough of them, and anything that was going, they'd have it if they could. The Gypsies got blamed for lots of things that Commoners done. Still, I think on the whole, the Keepers knew their Gypsies in their area. I mean I wouldn't have anything said against the Gypsies, the old Gypsies, because I knew them. We had lots of games with them and all that sort of thing. There used to be always one or two Gypsies coming down to our door to get a drop of milk or something or other, or a few potatoes, whatever we had to sell. We never had much trouble.

After they put them in the compounds they didn't move. They just stayed there, and it was really terrible. They herded them in there. I think we ought to have protested more than we did, but when the Forestry Commission came in, I suppose the commoners around was thinking 'Oh what are they going to do with us? We'll be next!' I suppose it was all that, and no-one protested.

I don't call it progress, as we come. I suppose it would have been a bit difficult for the people to accept them like we did. I don't think somehow they could really.

The commoning tradition

Almost all the families in Longdown worked in the fields and the woods to secure a living from a few animals and a small area of land. Each holding had a few cows, reared pigs and chickens and grew as much of the food it needed as was possible. They knew where to go when crops ran out, and they knew the local markets where they would sell their surplus for the cash they needed to pay the rent.

They worked together and socialised together, sharing the limited resources of their holdings and the labour they had at their disposal. They intermarried and were related in many ways. Much of the work they did for each other was unremunerated: one day's work was repaid by another, or by goods in kind. Together, they followed the cycle of

---

[8] Jack Humby, Forest Keeper

the seasons, ploughing, cultivating and harvesting by turn; taking the wealth that the soil and the Forest offered, and turning it back into the land.

After my father took on the tenancy they started to increase the stock: Father keeping more cattle and pigs, Mother with more poultry: butter, eggs – lots of poultry dressed for the table, vegetables to sell on the round in Southampton. Sometimes they would have a pig killed to sell on the round.

We had two fields that we used to plough of the twenty-eight acres. Two fields and one of them – it was a sandy old hill – I don't think it ever paid us a ha'penny. We always grew a few acres of corn, and now and again a bit of wheat, but it was oats mostly to feed the horses.

One field we used to keep for to grow mangels, vegetables, about 4 acres. My father used to do a bit of market gardening and later on he had a bit of a round of his own – wholesale. We had all sorts of vegetables in there: carrots, perhaps an acre of potatoes, and a lot of turnips. We used to sell more turnips off our holding then, than they would now in the whole of Southampton. Turnips were a really good business.

We used to plough it; but all the working was done by hand. A hoe, that's the best thing there is! I remember we always used to be out in the fields: ever so young, we'd go out and help. And perhaps someone would be shirking a bit; only in play more or less, Father'd pull up a turnip and throw at you, as much to say get moving. Then we'd throw one back!

After we got through to April we were planting out in the fields. We would grow just over an acre of the mixed vegetables and then, if we ran out, we had to buy something. We would always put in so many mangels and a few swedes - what ever we thought we might want - but they never lasted out the year. We had only enough to last till Christmas, or just after.

Our next neighbour, the nearest one at Fox Hills, at that time was one of the Smiths: Gilbert Smith. Later he had the Bold Forester. I used to go down to the Bold Forester when his father, Charles, was there and help them thrashing. We all used to help each other thrashing. We had the thrashing machine, the old steam engine. We'd only need it for half a day, or perhaps a few hours, because we didn't have all that amount to thrash, and we'd all help each other. We'd go round to the nearer ones and help them and then they would help us. There was no money paid, or anything.

Cutting hay at Acres Down, Minstead

We used to go to Bouvery quite a lot. I knew the people there. They were Scots: Scott by name – and they were Scots. They grew a lot of roots, mangels in particular, hundreds of tons, and hay and straw. When they were thrashing the straw, we would go and buy some. All the people did it – we were living in a different age.

They used to tie up bundles of straw on the back of the drum: six to a hundredweight. We reckoned we could get half a ton on a horse and forest truck. But, after we'd got the six up, half a ton, Mr Scott would say 'Any more room?' His sons would keep on throwing them up. They'd say, 'You say when we gonna stop.'

The mangels were to feed the cattle. We used to keep a dozen or so milking cows, and a few followers. So that was all to be done. Chaff the straw all up, grind the roots and mix it all up, and feed them. As long ago as I can remember, with my father, during the winter, after tea, we'd always have a game of draughts with him. Then, a bit later on when I was 9 or 10, he'd say, 'Now we've had a game of draughts, we'll have a game of chaff-cutting.' I used to go down and turn the chaff cutter handle while he fed the cutter.

All we kept on the Forest was cattle. We'd have a few extra heifers sometimes to make up a bit and sell them when they calved down and that sort of thing. But on the whole, we only kept the dairy cows and the followers. I was milking by hand, of course, and riding a horse – probably before I started school.

I was out every day to go and get the cattle on the forest - all through the summer, anyway (in the winter they used to come home, mostly). Then I would go out and have a ride. I used to be out every day. Always bare-backed. We had saddles, but I used to love bare-backed: you get no bother. Out in the field, catch her up, put the bridle on and you were away. And I loved that, going out and getting the cattle in, because you could start them on way home, hoping that they'd go on. Then you'd see something over there and you'd gallop across. Perhaps, you saw a bird, perhaps a kestrel or something like that, and try to find the nest sort of thing, look round and …. Where's the cattle?

Then we would go and buy an orchard - several orchards - almost every year, and sell the apples. Where the Butterfly Farm is now[9], there was quite a biggish orchard there. Another one (now that's all gone) a beautiful orchard - down where the new road has gone through Colbury now – Wingroves: we used to have all their orchards. They had a big house there. They'd take the few they wanted and we'd have the rest. Then there was another one up at Irons Lodge: they had apples that kept longer. Anywhere that had apples, we'd go and buy.

My brother and father and me used to pick them. We used to love picking them right up in the tops of trees; we didn't seem to have any fear. If you see another 2 or 3 big apples over there, you'd go over the top of the ladder and go on after them. As I said before, I'm sure in a way it was a lot happier times, a lot more contentment in the young ones.

---

[9] Most recently the Otter and Owl Centre

We used to take the apples around on our cart. We'd sell them in half bushel or bushel baskets, not by the pound. When I was 13 or 14, I used to load as many as I could get up. I had quite a few ordered. I went over as far as Woolston, over the floating bridge with the horse and cart. Cooking apples and eating apples. We had quite a few people would have a bushel of cooking and a bushel of eating apples.

Then we would go and cut bracken. One of the worst things that might cause trouble: if you went and cut someone else's piece of bracken. No-one dared do that! Some people used to have a part at Matley, perhaps split up into the roads that go through it. But we had two or three patches, just outside of Matley we used to cut. Then just outside of Foxhills, there was a big hill, and that used to be a lovely bit of bracken there. Then there was some up between where the Gypsies used to camp: a bit there. I mean, we'd scratch round every piece of bracken there was. And we would get the Gypsies to help us cut it.

The rule was, you couldn't get a ticket to cut the bracken in the Forest before the 26th September. So, the night before (we had bikes at that time), Father would say, 'Get up a bit sooner tomorrow morning and go up and get the ticket!' – in case someone else had taken it.

And then we would take a lot of leaves. Where we mostly went was Fernycroft. We used to rake the leaves all the way round the Forest. Me and my brother used to go down to Albert Humby's place in Purlieu and have a chat. We paid a ticket for two loads. He'd come along and say, 'I suppose that's number one isn't it?' Perhaps we'd had ten! Another man sometimes had some, but we used to have most of them. We had a deepish yard. We put the leaves in there and put our own manure on the top. Then, perhaps the middle of winter, we'd mix it all up – all by hand – by fork. Half the size of this house! Great big heaps of manure: to mix it up. It would all get rotted down.

Even when we cleaned out the ditches, we would put it out in little heaps. When we got to clean out the yard, we'd put two or three loads of yard manure with some of this from the ditches. All that had to go out, and be spread over the land. As boys, we'd take out the manure and we'd have perhaps five or six heaps up on a cart. And my father'd say we had to keep them four strides apart. If we put them a little bit less than that, we had to move them before we spread it. It seems ridiculous, but it was all discipline. I mean, we never disagreed with him, not in that.

Then, as long ago as I can remember, in February, we would go down on the Beaulieu Estate and get straw, swedes, and mangels and that sort of thing. We would always get plenty down on the Beaulieu Estate. I know nearly every field on the Estate.

Swedes and mangels they used to have in clamps and we'd go and buy them: tons and tons of them at this time of year. Perhaps, two or three times a week, we'd go down with two carts, to help each other. I would go with my brother, or occasionally a neighbour, and we would have one load each. If the swedes were still out in the field, they'd tell us to go on out and help ourselves.

Now potatoes! We would grow about an acre of potatoes. Sometimes we would have a good crop, and if we ran out potatoes then again we would go to Beaulieu, East Boldre. I knew nearly all the people down there at that time. Two or three of the Houses - Bob House and then there was Harry up a bit farther: they all grew a few potatoes and that. They put them in clamps and left them till now or a little bit later (February) and when we ran out we sound round and find out who had any – and we'd always find some.

I remember going with one of my brothers one night, nearly down to East End, to Bob House's father and mother. We had a wagon, and it was dark by the time we got there with the horse and cart. We loaded up, and then I suppose we had a cup of tea, I expect, or something – I can't remember all that – but I remember leaving there very late at night with this load of potatoes we had to come from there back to Marchwood – quite a journey.

We used to chaff hay and straw, but nearly all with gorse tops, fuzz tops. Hard work! The fuller you could keep the chaff cutter the easier it was. If it got a bit slack it jerked right round. The gorse was from January, through February, March, when other feed got short: that's when you done most of the gorse. That's when the prickle was a little bit softer. That's why you see the ponies in February, March time, nibbling.

We used to go and cut a bundle, a load: cut them up in big bundles half as big as those round bales, tie them up and that was a week's supply. We used to chaff up, perhaps one or two a day, whatever we brought home, with hay usually. We used to chaff a terrific lot: well 3, 4 or 5 horses and perhaps 8, 10, 12 cows, to feed on gorse. We used to do all that.

Another thing always done for the winter was pigs. We kept 3 or 4 sows and reared most of the young pigs for pork, selling them wholesale to the butchers in Southampton if the price was right. If not, we would have them killed and cut into joints which we would sell locally.

We would keep back two pigs for bacon. These would be kept until they were 30 or 40 stone 600-800lbs in weight. By this time they would be very fat. This was the order of the day in everything: beef, pork, mutton, lamb, all kinds of poultry. This was a very special thing for us children: we hoped it would happen on a day we were home from school. We had a man in the village who would come and kill the first pig, usually about the end of October, and the second during February. All would be got ready in the early morning. First, pulleys had to be fastened to a tree. A table, water and straw brought to the spot. We children were not to be allowed to see the killing, but afterwards we could see all the goings on.

First he would kill the pig, then place straw all over the animal. Then he would light the straw and keep moving it around until all the hair was gone. It would be washed before the dressing commenced: to take all the insides out to be eaten fresh – liver, lights, spare ribs and chitterlings. Then it was pulled up the tree to be left until the next day to cool off. For a few days we had lots of treats from different parts of the pig. You people today don't know what you missed! The next day the pig was cut in two sides, put in a strong box, plenty of salt rubbed in each side and left for about 2 weeks before being taken to be dried and smoked. This took about 2-3 weeks. Then there was plenty of fat bacon for us all.

World War I

The memories of the First World War are some of Dan's earliest. He saw the soldiers come and go, watched them exercise and march, and wondered at their magnificent horses, as they prepared to head to France and the trenches. From his child's eye view he was able to admire the Gordon Highlanders, and the companies of Indian soldiers with their turbans and strange customs, whom they invited home for Sunday tea.

He also saw his brothers and sisters sent off to war. Joe, his older brother, survived the whole four years from the age of 17, but was terribly damaged by the experience. His sisters were trained as nurses, and his other brothers, each in turn, were called up. When Charlie, his closest sibling, was sent off to war, Dan had to leave school at the age of 12, only to have him come back in 6 months as the war ended. Only Buffy, the oldest son, somehow evaded the grip of the War Department, and stayed out of the terrible conflict.

I was nearly 9 when war broke out. I can remember that they all knew that a war was coming up because we used to get, in the holidays, the Territorial Army coming out for manoeuvres and all that. I remember – and I can show you the spot – where I first heard that we'd declared war on Germany. Up in the field there, at Farringdon, we nearly always had a few young lads or young men then, come out camping. There was 2 or 3 of them out there on August 4th. I don't know what we'd been up the field for, well we was always walking round doing things. We were coming down from the field and one of them came out after work and told us that war was declared on Germany.

We'd never heard of anything before. It wasn't long before they started making a camp at Lyndhurst. Most people I've spoken to didn't realize how big the camp was at Lyndhurst. There was literally thousands and thousands of bell tents and, of course, marquees to keep their food and that in. It reached from Boltons Bench to Matley Wood and lots of Indian at Ashurst, all that area right down as far as it could go to where it was wet, down to the moor. You could get up on the hills round our place and see: it was like big white clouds.

That was where the main expeditionary force went from. I haven't heard anything much about it. They had roads in between. It was all horses at that time, nearly all Shires, Clydesdales: all the heavy horses, Suffolk Punches and all them: thousands of them. We had them almost every day around the school at Longdown. Our Governess let us go out to see them in their training.

You can guess what a mess it was during the winter. The first winter after they got the big camp, it was awful. Waste! Oh dear, dear. You'd never believe it. When one particular lot was going away they had to get rid of the food and clear it out, I don't think they could avoid it.

I used to go up with my oldest brother, Buffy, at night to clear up some of the swill at the camp, because you can guess that with all that lot they didn't know really what to do with it. I went up one night with him, I remember, I was about 10 or something. The track that we went on, all in the dark, between all the tents and that, it seemed to be a better road: great ruts had been before. I asked Buffy, afterwards, why they made the road up right through there, a better road now, it wasn't rocking so much. He said, 'Shh! Don't you say anything. 'Do you know what they filled them up with? Sides of bacon!!' All that went on during the war.

Bread! I've seen heaps of bread. There was a man down near Colbury Church; he had one of the fields there. He used to make a living out of selling this bread. I've seen heaps of bread in his field nearly as big as that barn. Heaps of bread. The army would bring it down and he'd sell it on for people to feed their animals, poultry and all that.

They were there for the whole war. They had to get the expeditionary force out because the Germans were nearly breaking through, and they were on manoeuvres all the time, seven days a week with all these horses. Wonderful sight it was to see the horses. We thought it was. They came down with all their big guns you see. The very big guns they'd have six of these big horses on.

For the ammunition they'd have four horses to pull what they called linvers, (the carts they carried the ammunition in). These poor soldiers, they had to sit upon the linvers. It was like a four-wheeled thing. One would sit at the front and one behind him. He'd have to hold on for his life because they'd go full pelt gallop across the Forest. Poor things: they had a job to hold on. I should think they had some sores like.

Another thing: when they were on these manoeuvres, they had men on horses; I forget the name they called them. They kept all the cattle and ponies one side of the river – say the Beaulieu River that goes right up through. There were 2 or 3 of the Kitchers, Bob House and then, of course, the Agisters, all them had quite a lot on horses. They were all in touch with each other, patrolling up and down, up and down all the time, keeping the ponies and the cattle out the way. We didn't know when our cattle were coming home if they were manoeuvring towards our part. They'd keep them the other side till they'd finished the manoeuvres. Our cows would be waiting to be milked. But we never had all that much trouble. I think they used to probably finish the manoeuvres middle of the afternoon, or late afternoon.

When they went away, we boys (we did get into trouble in the end – we did know better) would go out and pick up ammunition of all sorts and sizes out there. It was all over the ground everywhere. We had a sandpit: it was a wonder someone hadn't been hurt. We used to come back and light a fire, throw this in. We weren't angels in them days! Then we got found out and, of course, they stopped us then: they came to the school.

The other side of the railway between Beaulieu Road Station, a big area there, down to Matley Wood and right back in round to the railway. You could go out there after the war, several years after the war, you could have picked up a bagful of live ammunition. It was out there, they never cleared up. All that was one big swamp where their used live ammunition.

Saturday and Sunday before the very big lot went out - they thought they were breaking through, which they were - they were on all day. There was a big stretch of land outside the bottom gate near Foxhills, quite a big patch with a hill there. We used to take them down baskets of apples when they were around, and I remember on the Sunday it was full up with all these heavy horses. After they'd had manoeuvres: galloped round few miles and that, they'd bring them back and feed them. They'd have bars all along with poles through, to run a rope through. One horse each side facing each other, and they'd go and tip oats. They'd tip a ton out from here down to the end there. There was no shortage of anything.

After they'd had the manoeuvres and that, everybody would go out and clear up what was left. There were bagfuls of oats to clear up. Oats and oats, not like the rubbish we get today. The oats they used to grow were nearly like cornflakes, big oats. They used to have the best Scotch oats, always the best. All these horses, there must have been between 2 and 3 thousand, all these heavy horses it was a wonderful sight. The terrible thing was they went out and most of them were killed.

Then as time went on, we'd get more and more manoeuvres: all sorts. The Gordon Highlanders -- lovely lot of men. Great big wonderful Scots chaps, great big limbs. I can see them now on manoeuvres when we were going to and fro from school. The Governess would say, 'The army's coming, I'll let you go out for 10 minutes.' And we could all go out and watch them pass.

Highland regiment marching through Lyndhurst camp in 1914

They were all so pleasant to us, give us things and that. Marvellous! I can remember when, a day or two before they went to France, the Gordon Highlanders, were all round Longdown, right down all round there, thousands of them. They collected up together and they marched four abreast at that time: had the bagpipes and we followed them. It was marvellous. There must have been – well it was from Longdown to Beaulieu Road Station they were solid – that'll tell you how many of them, all in their kilts and that: wonderful sight. They went out and were mostly killed or wounded within a few days.

Then a bit later in the war – I think 1915 – we had the Indians come over with their mules and that. They were separate: at Ashurst (it's all built on now) both sides of the road at Ashurst, another campsite. We got to know quite a few of them. There was so many Indians and one British soldier that had been over there before the war, it was a recognized thing. I don't know how big the company was, but it was one man to each company. They used to come down to our place, my mother and a niece of mine would go up and invite them down for Sunday tea during the war. We got to know quite a bit about the Indians and their ways, from them.

Indian soldiers with mules at Ashurst

They used to bring us little bags of sweets, little nut things, they were queer little things, and throw them out to us, the Indians did. They couldn't speak English. You could hear all their lingo but we didn't understand that. We used to take out apples and we all seemed to, in the season, have plenty of apples. We all used to do a lot of picking in orchards so we always had plenty. I think other people used to do the same. You'd give them to them. You'd take a basket down and put down just out in the Forest and they'd come and help themselves.

The British had horses, but the Indians all had mules: hundreds and thousands of mules there was up there. You could hear them when they started. They used to come down for manoeuvres all round the school, pretty fearsome it was too. The old governess, when there was any manoeuvres on, she used to let us go out and look, see what was going on, see them creeping out of the bushes with big knives in their mouths. If we got the wrong side of them, we were afraid and wondered what would happen. We couldn't get back into the school.

If the sun was out you had to be careful not to get anywhere near their food because, if a shadow went over their food, they wouldn't eat it. Strange!

When the war started, first one brother was called up, he was 17. That was Joe, he went and then another brother – my step-brother, Ted – went. He was on the railway so he went straight out to France, but my brother Joe, he had 6 weeks training and he was out on the frontline in France: just 6 weeks training. He had a really rough time right through the war.

All this time more and more men were being called to the forces. Women were being taken for the Land Army. My first sister, Elsie, had stayed home and when the war broke out and she had to do some war work. They were pressing to get these young girls to go: she went as a VAD nurse. I think she done most of her training on me and my sister. We used to have to stay at night, she bandaged us all up. Tied up sort of thing. I suppose we enjoyed it, but that's what she done most of her training. Then she went somewhere here and then they sent her out to Alexandria.

The next sister, Nellie, started off a nurse and was nearly starved: she used to come home to eat. Me and my sister, who was younger than her: we used to carry food from Farringdon Farm up to the top of Hunters Hill every Monday night. She used to come home on a Monday and the food was to keep her through the week.

Rations for food were more difficult, though we in the country did not feel it quite so much as people living in the town. Although I was only young at the time, it left quite an impression on me. Up to the present time I do not like to see waste in any kind of way. How my parents fed us and gave us an interesting, good diet of food I do not know. Any way I can only say I done very well.

My brother, Buffy, tried all sorts of things to get out of it but, in the end, the last 12 or 18 months of the war, they did catch up on him and they put him in the Pioneer Corps: that was to do war work anywhere you like. We had an uncle in Staplewood Farm, so somehow or other Buffy managed to get himself landed there to do war work. He'd take his khaki off and put his civilian stuff on and do a bit of dealing. One day he was going up the lane and he caught sight of some army people up there. He thought, 'Oh I am in trouble now!', so he went right back down the road, got rid of his horse somewhere (I don't know where he left that), came right up round the back way, crawled in the house somehow, got into his army clothes. My uncle had thought to himself, I don't know what I'm going to say or do, but anyway he arrived and everything was alright. How he come to get it there I don't know, but he did.

Then of course, the last brother I had, Charlie, was called up right at the end. He'd been put back for 6 months and they called him up right on the end. That's why I left school early: I left when I was 12 and a bit. So I, who had already passed an exam, did not go back to school after the summer holidays. But it was not for long: the war ended in November. All my brothers came back. Joe went and worked for Buffy. Charlie came back on the farm so I had to find work. I went and worked for an old aunt and uncle of mine nearby.

My brother, Joe, was in the front line at 18. He was at Ypres, the Somme: had a terrible time. He survived: 2 or 3 of his mates were killed. One was the keeper woodman; he lived in the Halfway House. Parker the name was. Frank was the son and they were mates together out there with several others. They were in the Hampshire Regiment. You wonder how any of these came back and made any life at all.

Joe and me used to work together after he came back. Occasionally he'd talk about things, apart from that you didn't hear much. He told me once 'The worst thing' (of course being with horses, the same as all of us), 'At night time, you could hear a horse, just over there – crying, crying – where he'd been hit. And he said, 'And you daren't go out to him.' He said, 'If it had been a man, you'd go out and drag him in somehow. But a horse: even if you'd seen him, you daren't finish him off, because it would give your position away.' He said it was worse, really, to put up with the horses crying than it was the people.

Nellie Mansbridge in uniform

Towards the end of the war he came home on leave. This was in November a week or so before the war ended. Me and Father was out in the field pulling up mangles: beginning of November and they were nearly freezing as we were pulling them up. He arrived just before dark. I can see him coming down through the field now. We were expecting him that day because the police had come and told us he was on his way. We saw him come down the field. We had the horse and cart, but we left them out there, came in and and a good chat with him. We went back out and the cart was froze in. We had to hitch the horse out and bring him in. That was the beginning of November!

Joe came home filthy in every way: straight from the trenches. Mother said, 'Can't you change? He said 'I'm going into an outshed to change.' Mother asked him why; he said he'd tell her later on. He took off all his underclothes and put it out on a holly hedge, spread it all out there. He left it out there all night in this really hard frost and the next morning the trench bugs - they were as big as that[10] - and there was, I don't know how many, he had on him in his clothes, but one started moving – after it had been out in all that frost!

Then a cousin of mine, that was in the army out in France, came out to see us while my brother was there. This other cousin was there and they were talking. Joe said to him, 'I'm not going back out again.' He said, 'Don't be silly, Joe. You know what they'll do to you if you desert'. He said, 'Well, I can't take any more'. My cousin said, 'Well don't you worry. It'll be over before you get out there again'. He was home for a week and it was. But the terrible thing is, the cousin that was saying this, he had to go back out a few days before my brother, caught the 'flu and died on the boat. After he'd been right from the beginning to the end.

Town and country: a grocery round

Longdown's close proximity to the city of Southampton made it the ideal base for a grocery delivery business. Dan's mother's family were already taking groceries into the city when she was a child, but she expanded the business, and was joined by her husband, and later her children, in the regular trips to visit their customers in the western suburbs, and as far as the Kingsland Market.

The trade was based on eggs and chicken products, but also included butter, vegetables and fruit in season, fresh pork and woodland products such as pea sticks, bean poles and kindling. The family had their regular routes, and regular customers. Much of the produce was sold to order, and anything left over was sold to local shop keepers in the centre of town where Jessie could, in turn, do her own shopping.

---

10   He showed his finger nail

My mother always went to Southampton, twice a week to sell the produce: nearly always, Tuesdays and Fridays. Father used to go as well, but he wasn't such a good salesman as she was. And I've been going here and there, delivering something or other, since I was twelve. We went all the year round, didn't matter what the weather was or anything. We always had a bit of butter, not many eggs in the winter. We used to have to hide them or else some of our customers might come out and have a look round the cart.

How we got round, I don't know! I used to talk about this with my mother. We went with horse and cart, don't ask me how, because my mother would always stop and have a word with everybody – not long – but always had a word. With the horse and cart we used to do a bigger area than people would do now with a vehicle.

We weren't the only ones: there must have been hundreds going in from outside, all going into Southampton with their goods, whatever they had. Hundreds of them! People we knew. Govers and Tuffin's from Nursling We didn't know hardly where Nursling was, but we used to know people:. Some people from Lockerley: I didn't have the faintest idea where Lockerley was at that time, but we used to meet all of these people. We would go along the same road and have our own customers. No-one would go and cut across anyone. I've known 2 or 3 in the same road of a morning,

We would reckon to get in to Millbrook by half past eight. There was an old church with a clock right at the bottom of Regents Park, a very old church. And that clock was always going. Half past eight: summer or winter. If we were much later than that, we were late! We'd call all up through Paynes Road, through Howard Road, up Hill Lane, both ways of Hill Lane, back into Archers Road, Northlands Road, up the Avenue, back down to Avenue Road which was off the Avenue, back down through to London Road and down to Kingsland Square.

Sometimes in the winter, of course, it was dark by the time we got home, or dark on our way home, because we'd stop and have a cup of tea with people. Any of our customers: didn't matter which. We had two who were sea captains: one of them was on one of the big yachts, and the other was on one of the liners, I can't remember which one. Some were big houses, some ordinary small houses. There was a gunsmiths, Cox's of Southampton, up the Avenue – Winn Road.

We would do a shop if we had enough: if we had a bit to spare. We knew the people, at the shops: perhaps we'd had 10 dozen eggs, 5 dozen eggs, or whatever over after. We didn't want to bring them back, because there'd be some more when we got back, and we'd have a little bit of a bargain with someone.

I went with Mother for a long time, and we'd come right on down and end up on St Mary's Street, on Kingsland Square. While Mother was going to do a bit of shopping, I'd talk to the people. We knew nearly everybody in St Marys Street, because that's where Pondfords was. They were the only solely pork butchers in Southampton. We used to sell practically all our pigs to them. My brothers did it before me, but then they went their own way and I stayed there, on the holding. I used to take pigs in to the back place in St Mary's Street, where the Pondford's slaughter house was.

I remember one day, I went in with a load and I had a pony – a halfway horse – and she'd never 'back'. At Pondfords, you had to back down to the end of the alley. The old slaughterman was a great big, strong man, and I always used to get one or two of them to help me to push the horse back. So, I got right back to where we were going to unload them. This time – it only happened once – old Joe, the slaughterman, said, 'Hold her there a minute', he said. 'I'll drop the pin out and let the tailboard down.' Well, just as he got the pin out, I just couldn't hold her any more, she pushed me, took me and the cart, and the pigs were dropping out all down out in the street. They'd shoot you today, nearly! That happened: all that sort of thing happened.

On Kingsland Square, there were some people there and all they sold was bacon. It was lovely bacon and we used to always buy ours there, and they were nice people. Oh, I knew the father, and later, the son. And if we had a chicken or two over, we'd take them there and they'd sell 'em for us. And I don't know what happened, whatever they paid: that didn't matter. But I hadn't been down there for about 30 years, on Kingsland Square, and this is 5 or 6 years ago. I'd heard that they were still there - the Bacon Man – what we always called the Bacon Man: Underwood his name was.

I had some time (though I hate going into Southampton now: I hate it, because I don't know it like I used to). I parked right down the bottom of the High Street: the car park there. I walked up through High Street, on out through to Kingsland Square and I looked across and I thought to myself, 'Well, yeah, he's still got the same place there.' So I walked along. He had it all along on the pavement. I saw the son that was grown up: well he was 50ish then, I suppose. And he was sort of bent down and I stopped there for a moment, and he got up. He said 'Have you got a spare chicken?' After all that time! You know, and then we had a real good chat. It was marvellous: he just got up and he said, 'Have you got a spare chicken?'

Sometimes, I used to go in with my next brother on our own. I was only 7 or 8 and went with him – on the Saturday - and he used to do quite well. One day we were down what they called New Road, going down to the Six Dials, in Southampton. It was a terrible cold day and my brother was never very strong. We were just on our way home and we stopped at the last place. When we came out he started talking all rubbish. I didn't know what had come over him. I suppose the cold had taken over him. I didn't know what to do. I said 'Lay down in the bottom of the wagon.' and I covered him over with whatever we had, and I drove home from there. I was only about 8!

Early adult life

Dan's early working life was entirely based around the family holding at Farringdon, and his aunt's holding in Staplewood Lane, which runs off the Longdown Road. He worked with his father on the farm until his brothers returned from the war, and then for his Aunt and Uncle in the woods, coppicing and cutting small wood to sell in Southampton.

He married his childhood sweetheart in 1930, and they moved into a cottage on the Colbury-Beaulieu road. His older brother, Charlie, joined the Coldstream Guards, but Dan worked on with his father on the farm, and his brother, Joe, in the woods. As the Second World War approached the work in the woods was in decline. Joe went to work on the railways, and Dan started up a milk round in Southampton: a trade which he continued throughout the war.

When I was young we used to go round the village, meet the other boys, all that sort of thing: play football. I used to be in the Marchwood football team for a time. Then 4 or 5 of us would go into Southampton of a Saturday evening: go to the pictures perhaps. At that time we used to like cowboys. We'd cycle to Totton and get on the train; go in by train to Central Station as it is now. Then we'd walk wherever we wanted to go: the High Street or East Street, or wherever. Of course, we used to put our cycles in the station at Totton. I think it was only one night that we missed the last train, we had to walk out from there. When we got to Totton, they were all locked up, so we had to walk home and then walk back down to get our cycles the next day.

When my brother Charlie was called up right at the end of the war I had to leave school early. I left when I was 12 and a bit. Then it wasn't long before the war was over, and my brothers came back. When Joe came home he worked for Buffy for a time with horses: timber cart and that sort of thing, and sometimes doing a bit at home. Charlie came back on the farm, so I had to find work.

At that time I had an Uncle Jim and Aunt Sally, my father's sister, so I went to work for them at 1s 6d a week. They had a wood business at Dumpers Farm, selling all sorts of wood: logs, pea and beans sticks, posts of all sorts for the garden. At that time there used to be a lot. Nothing in the woods was wasted.

I used to go from Marchwood to Southampton every day of the week except Sunday, with wood – all sorts of wood. Kindling: you bundle up 25 of these small 'nickies'–kindling wood – and put a whip round them and tie them up. I went with this old lady: we used to take two loads, a load each. Partly we took orders and then we'd go and sell the others if we could. I've carried half a load of pea sticks on my shoulder – I was only 13 years old, mind. Then I had my father's horse and cart.

I had an old mare, Ginger, that I used. Well, we nearly used to live together sort of thing. You could do anything with her: she was a marvellous horse. She was 35 when she died, and we used her up until she was 34. It wasn't a really hard job -- you had a load of wood whatever: 8, 9 or 10 hundredweight - so she wasn't worn out in that way. I used to walk to Southampton and ride back. This meant I was away from home almost 12-14 hours a day. But I enjoyed it and I learned a lot about selling things which has lasted all these years.

Through the winter, I hardly ever saw any daylight at home. I've driven back to the farm and, nearly always through the winter, it was dark. I didn't need to do anything. I'd come on home and this old horse, Ginger. She knew her way, right up a Forest track. I had got to the top gate and suddenly felt a jolt. Perhaps I was asleep: she'd stop at the gate. She always brought me home. Never ever did she go astray.

Then the time came and we retired her for a twelve month. Father said, 'We'll keep her another year.' Then, I suppose, it got on before the winter, he said, 'I don't think we ought to try to keep her another winter.'

He rung up Pat the knackerman and arranged it. I took her and tied her on a gate. I didn't want to see. All we wanted to see was the end of her and that she wasn't taken off. I suppose we hung around the yard there for quite a long time, I don't know whether it was morning or afternoon. Anyway the man, the boss who used to come out and shoot them, something went wrong and he sent out this young man. He came up to us. He'd seen the horse there. He said, 'I've come in place of Patty to get this horse.' Father said, 'Well what about it?' The man said, I'm not going to do it on my own. I want somebody with me. I want somebody to hold her.' I was listening and thought, 'Dear, dear. What's going to happen?' In the end Father said, 'You'd better go on down.' It nearly broke my heart! I can see it now: I had to hold her while he shot her.

After I had been working for my uncle and aunt for just under 2 years, my brother Charlie joined the Coldstream Guards, so I came back to work for my father. My uncle had already got Joe to work for him. After a time, my father went back to the wood business, showing my brother and myself how to go on with it: thinking that my brother would carry on the business of my Uncle Jim as he was getting beyond it. Joe knew about wood: how to cut wood up, but he didn't know much about in the copse, woodwork: how you cut beansticks and all that, because that's where you made the money. Father had already been on that for years since his early life, so in the morning after we finished milking, they used to go on down in the copse, so my brother could get an idea of how to go on: he was marvellous later on. I used to clean out and go down to meet them down in the woods: I knew where they were.

So we were now doing farming, and all three of us filling in our spare time in the woods. Sometimes my older brother, Buffy, would ask me and Joe to help him out in his hire cart business. So I had a variety of jobs, but most of my time I was working with my brother, Joe. I would go to the old place most evenings after I had finished work on the farm, to help him sawing logs on the saw bench. I've been down there at 12 or 11 o'clock at night plenty of times: then had to get up and ride a bike home.

Charles Mansbridge (seated) in the Coldstream Guards

It must have been 1930 when I got married to Ivy Smith. She was about 20, I should think, when we got married. She was that much younger than me - between 4 and 5 years. We had known each other for a long time. I mean, we went to school together: I knew all the ones at school. She only lived about half a mile from where I lived. On the Barker Mill Estate in Longdown. There's two blocks of three houses: three houses in one. Her grandmother was one of the first tenants to go in when it was new. I think it was one Sunday School treat when we first really got together – to know each other.

After she had finished school she stayed home and worked with her father. They had a holding and they used to keep a few cattle, the same as we did, and they used to do hire cart. Same as we did wood to help out, they did road repairing and all that sort of thing. They later kept the Bold Forester: her grandfather passed it over to her father.

We moved into a house on the Colbury-Beaulieu road when we got married. I used to go across the fields, I suppose half a mile something like that, to Farringdon every night, winter and summer – well, winter more – to rack up and see if the cattle were alright. My father was getting on a bit then, so I used to always go across and go in and see if they were alright.

The night we got married we walked from my wife's people at Longdown to our own house. We had about half a mile to walk. It was pouring with rain and we got soaked through. When we got to the house, my brother-in-law – my sister's husband – had been and tied the doors up. Every one! I had no pocket knife in my best suit. We kept on fiddling around – we didn't have a torch. We had everything ready inside to light the candle to start off with. That was always the first thing: you lit the candle before you lit the light, because there was no electric. It was a good joke – we could see it afterwards, but not that night!

I worked together with my brother for years, after he had gone to live with my Uncle Jim and Aunt Sally in the winter months. Then Joe got married and he took over. My old uncle died and old Aunt Sally, that was my father's sister, lived on a bit longer. Joe stayed there in the same plot. It was an old thatched house, but they've pulled that down. It was on the Barker Mills estate, and they built a new house there: it's a bungalow now.

His wife died fairly early, and his second wife is still living there. But they took the land away when my brother died.

That old uncle of mine, in his young days, used to do a tremendous lot of coppicing. He used to employ a lot of boys. At one time, so my father told me, including the boys, he employed nearly 40 on wood, on that small piece of land. I went in when he was beginning to go back a bit, but when he was in his high production, he had a lane going down into Dumpers, that was all brick: I can see it now, that lane: one side would be pea sticks and bean sticks all packed in tidy. The other side, clothes posts and everything to do with wood – only everything to do with wood. Clothes props and clothes posts, all of it: junk wood. Every time there was a load or two went away, one of the boys had to go up and sweep it. It was always swept and kept clean. A brick or two out of place, they'd take them out and put them in. I suppose he didn't pay these boys very well, but there was 4 or 5 used to live in with him.

At that time, everything was done as it should be done. We used to reckon the copse had to be cut every 9 or 10, 11 years at the most. Then you had clean bean sticks, pea sticks – thousands of them. Mostly hazel: we liked to get hazel. I used to take it round with the horse and cart. We tried to push in a few oak, because you wanted to clear up the woods. They'd say, 'Don't bring any more of those oak!' They used to like hazel: it was the best.

I never used to do much, in the way of spars, but my father could make spars really professionally. Spars are what you use for thatched rooves: the stake. You point them at both ends. So he used to do all that, everything which came from the woods. I expect on Barker Mill Estate down there, during the winter, there was perhaps up to 5 people that used to have their own business. Probably they employed up to 100 men and boys.

They cut it all the winter, before the nesting season started. Then probably all through the summer they'd get wood, cord wood we call it, get loads of it in for the winter. My uncle was always fully employed on wood alone. The 12 acres of Dumpers Farm was down to grass, but he'd buy the woods. Perhaps he'd buy 50 acres of woodland or whatever he thought he could deal with. If he could possibly cut it during that first year he would, because he'd already paid for it and he wanted the money back.

The next year he'd buy some more wood somewhere else. If there wasn't any on the estate he'd go further afield. Of course a lot of the cord wood for logging would come from the Forest, anywhere there was anything going. They were always fully employed.

That was the early part of my life. Later on when the work in the woods got less, Joe found other employment on the railway and I stopped with Father. I came back and helped on the farm when I was about 15 or 16, and started going to Southampton again with my mother. We started up a bit of a milk round, and it went on from there. That was nearly a fulltime job – milking the cows, bottling the milk, going to Southampton every day. That was a horse and cart in the first place. Then we bought a new little van. I think it was 1930/31 something of that. I was going to go in the war, and then they said that my father was too old to carry on the place, so I stayed.

I kept on the milk round until 1945 or '46. Brown & Harrison Dairies were buying up everyone after the war. I was really sorry afterwards that I did give it up, but I suppose it would have come sooner or later. Otherwise, we'd of had to have a plant put in, which wouldn't have been worth it. Brown & Harrison kept coming to me and asking me if I'd sell and, in the end, I did I suppose: when they offered what I thought was enough. After I sold, they used to come and collect on the lorries.

After that I only used to go round, mostly once a week. Until a couple or 3 years ago, I've been going all round Southampton once a week. I had quite a round with all sorts of vegetables. I'd grow a bit and buy some, which we'd always done. If we were short of anything, any market gardeners or anything like that, we'd go to them. We knew – well everybody knew each other in whatever you were doing.

World War II

The Second World War had some profound effects on the New Forest. Not only was the area used to build airfields, gun emplacements and bombing ranges, it was also close enough to the port of Southampton to be within the dropping zone for attacks aimed at the city and a base for the D-Day embarkation.

49

From their vantage point on the western shores of Southampton Water, residents of Longdown were able to watch the bombing of the city which, at times, lit up the night sky. They were also surrounded by targets for the bombers, with searchlights and gun emplacements all along the western shore. Dan and his family were bombed out of their cottage, and moved into Farringdon with his parents. However, they were far luckier than some of the families that he knew and served in Southampton where bombing raids forced the population out of the city on a nightly basis.

I worked on the farm at Farringdon until I took it over in '39, but I lived across on Colbury Beaulieu Road, in a house there. It was November '41, I think, when we got bombed out. We didn't get very much bombing in the early part of the war; it was later when we got bombed out. That particular night – it was a terrible night – they were dropping them everywhere: bombs dropping all the time. They came round and dropped these flares, at about half past five, I suppose. They dropped a stick of bombs right up through and I was backing the car out, because the wife's people had a shelter up at Parkers Farm, only a little way up the road, and we were going up there. The wife had one of the boys (the little one) in her arms. Of course, you didn't have no lights on or anything. Before we could go in the shelter where the wife's people were, they were coming round again. We could hear the bombs, so we dived under the table. Then they came back round again and dropped a stick of bombs and one dropped in front of us. The blast went the other way, or else we wouldn't have been here.

We had search lights in the farm there, just at the bottom of the hill, and we had anti-aircraft guns just out in the lane. I expect they were after the search lights. If the fighters could dive round and put everything out of action, the bombers could come in and do what they liked. I suppose probably they were after the magazine, or the docks and all round there.

I thought they'd hit the farm, because all sparks and everything went up, you see: I was worried. We couldn't do anything because it was hell let loose. There was guns and shrapnel everything.

The bombing went on until about half past eleven, twelve o'clock, I expect it was. Then, when it eased up a bit, I thought, I've got to go over and see what's happened. I was going along a track that I knew by the hedge: it was terrible mud and the ditch was full up with water. I happened to look up and Southampton was on fire. You could have sat and read a newspaper at Marchwood quite easily. I saw a plane come in from the Forest, and I saw the bomb come out. I ought to have known it was nowhere near me but, after you get a bit scared, you do anything. I dived in the ditch of water. After I heard the whistle was gone, I looked up through the hedge and I saw it hit Ranks Mill. That was the last bomb of that night.

Rank Flour Mills in Southampton after a bombing raid

I could see that the house was alright before I got there, so it wasn't a direct hit on the house, but just in the field 100 yards away there was a clump of fir trees. It had dropped in there and this bomb had sliced the trees as it went down through: sliced off all these big trees just like a piece of matchwood. I had cattle sleeping there. I can't remember whether it was 2 or 3 killed and 2 or 3 more I had to have destroyed in the morning because they'd been hit.

The bombing brought the ceilings and all that in our cottage down: we never went back there again. We moved over to Farringdon. We had a caravan first of all. The cottage is gone now, it was pulled down.

There wasn't any milk hardly the next day from the ones that we did have left. Well, there wasn't any sense to anything for a day or two, not in Southampton or anywhere. Everything was so chaotic that no-one really wanted anything, you had to wait a few days and pick up the pieces again and then go on. Of course, everybody was the same. After that bad night that we had, they came back again each weekend. Southampton was literally empty of people, no-one was left.

We carried on deliveries in Southampton all through the war. My nephew used to come with me on the milk round any time he'd like. He went to Taunton School but if he could get away any time he'd be on the milk round. One day, quite recently, he told my son, 'I was with your father in Balmoral Road, Southampton, one day in the war and he mended four punctures. He had to get underneath and mend four punctures in that one road and it was pouring with rain all the time.'

It was impossible to get a tyre or tube. If there were holes through the cover, you'd cut a bit out of another old tyre and put it underneath. There was a garage in Waterloo Road, Southampton, who were our customers as well. I was there one day, the tyre was going down. I said to the chap that was there that I knew like, 'I've got a puncture. I can do a few round here, walk round here, if you'll mend it for me.' When I come back, he said, 'Mr Mansbridge, I think it's about time you had a new tube. I said, 'I'm waiting for that one you said that's been on order for about six months.' He said, 'I counted and you got 78 patches on that tube.' That was only on one wheel, I don't know how many was on the others.

You just couldn't get them, not even for emergencies. Milk was an emergency you see. We could get extra petrol if we got low. You had to give account why and all that sort of thing. People don't realise. We got through that all right in a way, the war. We managed on our own then for about 5 years.

But yet we didn't worry too much. As long as we could live, that was all that mattered really. You had to go round and try to pick up the bits and pieces, that sort of thing. You managed it somehow.

You didn't know really what you were doing or who you'd lost. People that owed you a bit of money and that, they were bombed and killed: several of my customers were. One house in particular, very nice people, right up the top of Hill Lane, they used to have quite a lot off of us. I suppose you had more trust in people then than you have today, especially during the war. They owed me quite a bit. I went there and, Oh dear, it was sad: they had a direct hit on the house. The whole family went: lovely people they were too.

Southampton firemen tackling fires after a night's bombing

Several nights when they had the Blitz, the next morning Southampton was empty, because they were afraid of the bombing. They'd go and stay the night all out round the outskirts: Nursling and all round that area. The roads were full up with people, nowhere even to lie down of a weekend: that's when they came bombing mostly. They were standing up and talking all the night, just to get away from the town. About half past 12 or one o'clock, the bombers would be gone back.

Sunday mornings I used to go and drop the milk and hardly see anyone. I used to get in there fairly early, to get out before the bombs started again. I remember one Sunday morning I was going in and I could only get as far as Redbridge: the road were absolutely blocked with people with all their bits and pieces, carrying it on prams out of the city. I had to wait until they thinned out a bit before I could get into Southampton.

When I got in there, there was a few left. I dropped the milk round - hoping, I suppose. We lost some of it, but no-one worried as long as you could keep going and do something. I wasn't the only one, there was lots of people selling milk at that time. Because the wholesalers had cut the price, quite a lot of people started retailing their own. Everybody carried on, everybody helped each other, it didn't matter, whoever it was. I've been in there when they've been all up overhead, dropping bombs and then they'd dive right down and go up a road, machine gunning everything. Terrible, terrible. I've seen awful things.

I was coming down Shirley Avenue, near Shirley High Street, one morning and it was dark (I used to get in there early). I thought, whatever's that? There's something in the road (because you'd no lights or anything). I pulled up and a bomb had dropped right in the middle of the road and there was a car gone right down in. There was no-one in the car, only just the back of the car sticking up out. I don't know what happened, how they got out or what.

In the same road, I came down there again one morning, only just getting light. There was a milkman that I knew; we worked together if I was short like. He came running out and I said, 'What's on?' 'Don't worry what's on,' he said. He opened the door and jumped in and said, 'Go like mad somewhere.' So I went on down and as I went in round the back, it was still twilight, and this old gentleman was out there poking this thing about that was hung up in a tree. It was a landmine hung up in a tree. He didn't know what it was: he was out there poking it about with his stick! It didn't go off, otherwise the whole of Shirley Avenue would have went! The whole lot would have gone up. The same night, one had dropped farther up, off St. James Road, and it had blown 150 houses down - a terrific area was devastated.

Anyway, we went on down and when the All Clear went, they let us go back up and they'd just dismantled this thing. They had it in two parts and they were bringing it out. It had been dropped by parachute and it was hung up in the big tree.

Another time I was in Hill Lane: that was mid morning, and I had a lad used to go round and help me. We were just pulled up, we could hear them having a battle up over the clouds. It was low cloud and they were machine gunning right up overhead. Then one dived down through the cloud. There was one of the barrage balloons only just over the road. It dived down and machine gunned and set that on fire, then went back up again.

Then there was another skirmish going on up above the clouds. There was a bit of a clearance and a bomber came in and we thought it was going to be nearer us than it was, but it was up in the Avenue. This lad of mine he said, 'Look! Bombs!' and he run and tried to get in this lady's door and he couldn't. He hit his shoulder up against it, he was so scared. I stopped there and it hit St. Luke's Church in the Avenue. The whole church, you could see it go right up in the air, all in pieces.

Yet it seemed if there was a terrible raid on, within a day everything was cleaned up (except when there was a house devastated - well they couldn't do that). All the other fragments were cleaned up, the people must have got to work. The next day you'd hardly know, apart from the devastation you could see everywhere.

They were trying to hit the docks -- all round there. That's what they were after. Then probably there'd be some gun emplacements and they'd tried to get them as well. There was one up at Fernycroft – Yewtree - big heavy guns they were. They never hit them, but they went all round there. Then we had them doodlebugs: terrible things[11]. We had one when we were at Farringdon. We saw it early one morning: floated along and went and landed in a field not far away. Just floated past us.

One day there were several of us there at home, and we saw these planes. There had been no sirens, no, nothing. They came in from Beaulieu way looking from where we were. There were 11 of them, all in formation.

---

[11] V1 flying bombs.

They got nearly over the docks and I suppose something turned up, and all the guns started, but it was too late: they'd got in past all the defences. That was Blenheim bombers that the Germans had captured. They didn't recognize them! They came in and they did a terrible lot of damage all round Southampton, round the docks. The submarines at Woolston: they hit them. Lots of direct hits they had, because no-one knew. When the guns opened up they'd already dropped their bombs, and they were gone. I don't think they brought down any of them.

We had no defences - nothing – here, except the Home Guard. I was in the Home Guard. I was an LDV, Local Defence Volunteer, at first. We walked round - two of us together - at night time, just to see and that sort of thing. Then they brought in the Home Guard and we had some of the old soldiers in charge. We had a Colonel Venning. He was in charge of the whole lot around Hythe and all up through there. In a way they knew what they were doing – trying to do – to make some sort of defence. When we went in the Home Guard we had a uniform, after a bit. First we only had sticks, our walking sticks or whatever. What we'd do with them I don't know! Anyway, then they let us carry our shotguns for a time.

Then after a time we all had rifles issued and had a clip of our own each, so we carried that about and we thought we could shoot anything! We had 4 rifles issued and 4 sets of ammunition clips. There'd be 5 in a clip. We used to meet every week at the hut where the Butterfly Farm[12] is now: that was our headquarters. There was always 4 at least every night at the hut: 2 out to walk round and 2 in. We carried on like that for 5 or 6 weeks. Then, one night, this old commander asked us for all our ammunition back. We were all a bit disgruntled about this. When we got there he said, 'I'm sorry to tell you men, you've got the wrong ammunition!' It wouldn't fit in the rifles, you see, but it was sealed and we'd never tried it! From then on, we had the right ammunition, but we never had to use it. Of course, we used to go for practice shooting and all that sort of thing, but we never had any contact with the enemy.

They had to have a bit of fun, although there was a war on ……all sorts of things we used to get up to. Bob House – he was a bit of a character: all

---

[12] Most recently the New Forest Wildlife Park at Longdown

the things that he used to do! A lot of the people came to the forest: they were evacuees, of course. Bob and they down at East Boldre, they had more down there, I think. They used to play tricks on them, you know. Try to get them out and frighten them at night and all that sort of thing. They drove these donkeys into the gravel pit, down there. Shut them in like, when they knew that these evacuees were there. They were in the Home Guard you see. They made them rustle all out through, made the people run for their lives: they thought it was the Germans coming!

Then Bob never got on with the Ministry. They came round during the war and asked him what was in each field: they wanted to know what he was putting in each field. They went right round the farm and he had a small field - 5 or 6 acres - there left. They said, what you're going to put in here then? He said, 'Rhubarb seeds.' He told me the Ministry wrote it down. I don't know if they ever came to check up; I never knew that.

Old Bob he could never get on with the Ministry very well. He went up to Lyndhurst: that was the Headquarters. Food – if you wanted anything you had to go up to HQ at the Grand Hotel. He said, 'I went up there to find out something about something. There they was, all sat back with their cups of tea and one thing and another. They wasn't interested in what I'd come for, or anything. So, I said to them, "I come up here to get some information and I didn't know it was an eating house!"'

He was a good man, in every way. He wouldn't put up with any nonsense, you couldn't tell him, he was like all Foresters, a bit stubborn I suppose. That's how they survived all the time.

They came to me at Farringdon and told me what I had to put into the fields. One field I had to put some oats in. I tried afterwards and I got in touch with them again somehow and I said, 'I can't get any seed.' They said, 'Well you'll have to get some somewhere.' I tried everywhere. I went down to Bob's and I said, 'Here, have you got any oat seed left?' He said, 'Yeah, I got a sack left, I'm sure. We're finished drilling today, I'm sure I'll have some over.'

So, next day I went down again and he had these oats, whatever he had over. He had just enough for me to do this field. I asked him about settling up, he said, 'Wait and see if they'll grow first.' I went back several times. In the end he said, 'Look, the poor always helps the poor, forget about them.' So I never paid him for the oats. That crop of oats! I've never seen a crop of oats anywhere like it. I knew the field had always had plenty of farmyard manure you see. We even had a job to cut it, it was so thick. I always think about that.

When I think about it, it seems so terrible now. In two wars, the people – didn't matter what station in life they're in – everybody helped each other, in any way. There was nothing people wouldn't do for each other. I don't think that you would get the young men to do what they've done in the last wars, not knowing what they do now.

Buffy Mansbridge

Buffy was the maverick of the Mansbridge family. He was born in 1893, the eldest son of George and Jessie, and Dan's older brother by 13 years. He had his own way of life – mostly as a horse and cattle dealer – and his own way of living it.

He did not share his brothers' fate in France, but spent the last two years of the First World War, in the Pioneer Corps at Longdown. He was well known in local pubs where he liked the odd drop, and he was well known across the channel in France where he took his animals to sell. He spent his life with horses, buying and selling them, as well as riding them. He was good at getting people to help him, either in terms of work or money, yet he was universally liked and respected by the people who knew him.

My eldest brother was Buffy. Well I mean, that's what everyone called him. Don't ask me why we called him Buffy. William his name was. He was a dealer. You say about dealers now, some people think it's a nasty word, but I guarantee 50, 60, 70 years ago you could go to anyone down round East Boldre, East End - anywhere like that - they all praised Buffy up and they always had a good word for him: he was one of the fairest dealers that they knew.

He was a character! He lived at Longdown: Animal Corner we used to call it, because you would never knew what you were going to meet down round there. You go from Colbury past the Butterfly Farm that was, wind your way on down there and his was on the right the last place on the right before you'd turn into the old school. It's still there now.

I tell you one thing that I remember first about him (even politics weren't vicious like they are today). This is about Buffy and my next brother, Charlie. We had a friend: he was a real friend. He always liked to come down to our place. He was something to do with the banks, I don't know quite what. He lived up in the village at Longdown, you know, and he was a gentleman. At that time, we had the only two ways of getting rid of rats, was to either to ferret them or trap them. He use to like ferreting them. He used to come and spend a lot of time with us, and he had a dog, named Dandy, a little Jack Russell. A lovely little thing it was, and the dog used to come as well. I've never seen a dog work like he would. He'd grab a rat and throw it back over his shoulder and wait for the next one, and he would throw one after the other.

And, of course, the dog used to sometimes come back down to us, though he was the biggest part of a mile away, but very often we'd see him out there running round. The dog had come down and it was just before the election and everybody at that time used to have ribbons; we were liberals and he was a Tory, the friend up there. So they got hold of the dog and wrapped all these ribbons round the dog, and the dog went on home. This man, if he wanted Buffy or my other brother to take anything, a letter or anything, he'd know roughly what time they would be along. So he came out the next morning, and I suppose they had quite a lot of ribbons on the horse, and he said, 'Hello Buffy', he said 'I see you didn't use all the ribbons on the dog!'

Buffy would go round and buy calves take them on to market -- ponies - anything there was going. He'd buy any live animals, horses, cattle, calves, a lot of calves, pigs. If he was anywhere and he saw a cow and calf, he'd buy them: always used to be doing that.

He'd go and buy all down round Beaulieu. Everybody all round Beaulieu, East Boldre and that, they all knew him. He'd buy them there and take them onto market or, I suppose, if he wanted one or two ready to kill, he'd keep them. He was solely a dealer all his time. I don't know whether ever he made much money. He was the only one in the family was like it in that way.

I remember coming back from Beaulieu, because I used to go round with him, only just for a ride. We were coming up from East Boldre, at nine, half past, at night in the winter, with a horse and cart and we had to get home. We saw a chap all in the dark, coming along before we got to the slope where you come up to Hatchett Pond. Buffy had an open truck with some rails round, and this chap hopped up over and got in the back. After we got moving a bit, this man that he picked up must have moved or something: he didn't realize there was an old sow up the back. Buffy hadn't said anything about it. The chap jumped straight out of the truck and ran off. He was scared out of his wits!

Buffy used to do a lot with pork up there at Longdown. He used to rear them up on barley or what ever and sell them. Though there was a big gap between us, he knew roughly what time I used to be going into Southampton every morning: he'd be always out, 'Oh, take this half a pig or calf,' (all dressed like), into one of the butchers in Southampton. That's what I mean. He never paid me for all those things I used to do. He might give me a sixpence now and again, I don't know. He always had a lot of stuff of all sorts there, keep buying and selling and that was solely what he done.

At that time we were rearing a lot of calves for beef. I never liked to ring him up, because if I rang him up and said 'I want's a couple of calves,' he'd land up here with eight or ten. Somehow we used to have a deal, 'Ah,' he'd say, 'Another one or two won't make much difference.'

He would go up to Wales and buy these Welsh Cobs. They were a very good type – dual purpose. I remember one day, I don't know how he got the telegram through to me and my brother: would we go to Beaulieu Road station and fetch some of these Welsh Cobs? Unbroken! It was dark by the time we got them. I remember we took a biggish horse, a heavyish horse, and it had one or two on each side. You can guess what a time we had coming back from Beaulieu Road, getting back across the Forest and all.

Another time, I was going up on the round one morning and he came out and stopped me. He said he wanted a lift down to Totton. So we took him. We let him down at the square and he said, 'I'm off up to Wales'. He was going up to Wales to buy ponies - go up and buy a truck load. He didn't have the fare to get back, so I gave him my half a crown.

About six or seven years ago, his grandson came over from Australia (one of his daughters went out there. We hear from her quite often and this grandson came over). He was about sixteen: I took to him, and he took to me -- more than ever you would know. We couldn't keep away from each other! Either Buffy had to bring him up here or I had to go down there. So, I went down there one night. I walked on in. I said 'How are you tonight then, Buff?' 'I feels pretty rough.' he said, 'I don't know what's the matter.' His grandson said, 'Uncle, if someone said there was a bottle of whiskey up at the Crown and Stirrup, he would be off like a shot!'

We went right on talking. This grandson's name was Andrew - and I said 'You any good at maths?' Andrew said, 'I don't know. What do you want to know?' I said, 'It was roughly sixty five years ago: I wonder how much interest you'd get on half a crown? I tell you what, if you can get the interest, we'll go halves!' So he said 'What's this all about?' Buffy then said, 'What you on about?'

So I said, 'Well look Buffy, you borrowed half a crown off me about sixty five years ago and I was wondering if I could get a bit of interest on it now, so that me and Andrew could share it.' He said, 'Did I never pay you that back then?' I said 'No you didn't, apart from other things as well'. 'Ah well', he said 'It's not worth worrying about that today, is it!'

Again, about Buffy, I don't know how old he was, he must have been between 40 and 50 I suppose – I wasn't all that old – when he had the worst accident with a horse. He was down at Dibden Bottom, coming out of Claypits Lane. I suppose the horse threw him and he couldn't get his foot out of the stirrup. He was dragged from there up to Ipley Crossroads. You've never seen such a mess! We never thought he'd live. He always carried a lot of scars; you could see them right up until he died. Unbelievable how he got over it. That's why I hardly ever used a saddle: I was always rode bare-back.

Of course, he used to like his drop. He was very friendly with the Pennys at Lyndhurst. I knew Ted very well, and his father, Charlie, was about Buffy's age; they were quite friends. They had a bit of a do up at the Trusty Servant. It got on late about half past twelve and Buffy said, 'I'm going to make me way on back home'. Ted said he and his father would stop and clear up. Buffy had his old T model Ford up there – that's what he had for years. When they came out an hour later, Buffy was still there. He had the starting handle through the back wheel: turning the back wheel. He said,

'I don't know. I can't get to start her up.' Young Ted said, 'Alright, you get in and I'll start her up for you.' He took him round and started her up, and Buffy drove on home. How he got home, I don't know!

A final thought

I ought to go back a bit about my parents: I never quite finished. There was a little bit I wanted to say about them. Every night, we'd have prayers before we went to bed. Mother would read a little, just a little bit out of the Bible and then she would have a little prayer and then we all said a little prayer together. I always used to kneel at my father's knee, always, and the little prayer I'll try to remember.

"Father hear my prayer before I go to rest
It is your little child who waits to be blessed
Lord help me every day to love thee more and more
To try to do thy will to worship and adore
Look upon me Lord ere I lie down to rest
'Tis your little child who comes to be blessed"

That was the prayer you know. Then as soon as we'd had the prayer we all went to bed, we didn't have to be told, I don't think, very often.

Len Mansbridge: 1917 to 2011

The Homestead: early childhood

Len Mansbridge was born at the Homestead in Longdown on 17th August 1917. His father had taken the property in 1915 as a rental from the Barker Mills Estate that owned all the land from Hunters Hill up to Twiggs Lane. He was brought up on the holding where his father taught him to understand the Forest, to handle horses fearlessly, to deal fairly with his neighbours, local traders and dealers – and to respect the local gentry. Like many young commoners of the time – and to the present day – he could ride almost before he could walk.

His grandparents, and his uncle Dan, lived a mile up the road at Farringdon. As a boy he learned the old skills of the forester, and the dutiful hard work of the small holder from his grandparents. These have stood him in good stead throughout his life and enabled him to develop his own style of survival and commoning to the present day.

It must have been while my father was in the army he took the Homestead at Longdown. That was a house and a few buildings and there was about 12 acres of land: it was from the Barker Mills estate. They paid the rent twice a year – Lady Day and Michelmas Day – and the rent for the house and the land and the whole lot was the big sum of £15 a year. He must have taken it in 1915 because my elder sister was born in 1915, I was born in 1917, and we were both born at the Homestead.

Before he took it, the Homestead was a shop, apparently. If you look at it, you can see the difference – there's a front door; then there's a side door which was the shop. I think it mainly sold groceries and, I suppose cigarettes and sweets. I don't really know why, but he never carried on the shop.

The land down through Longdown until you get almost to The Bold Forester was all Barker Mills. It still is. Their land reached from the other side of Hunters Hill - at the top of Hunters Hill there was a a big house; we always called it the Mansion. If I remember rightly, the gate is still there, just a wicket gate. That's where the Barker Mills sisters lived. I remember them and I remember Lady Barker Mills - the mother. They were rather tall people and always wore black right down to the ground. If we met them, we'd go to the other side of the road. It was the same with the vicar that was at Colbury in those days; we'd go the other side of the road and say 'Afternoon, Sir' or whatever.

The Homestead in 2010

All that land on the right-hand side from the top of Hunters Hill right down to Twiggs Lane, had no Forest Rights. They always said it was 'edged off the Forest'. I would think nearly all of those people who lived in the cottages there had a house-cow. I suppose what happened, you had the Forest alongside and you opened the gate and out they went! As I say, the rights were not recorded then; not in the Atlas.

My grandparents lived at Farringdon Farm, a couple of miles away. There was a little chapel at Longdown, opposite the school, a Wesleyan

Methodist; and my grandmother was a caretaker and guardian of that, as well as a Sunday school teacher. Sunday mornings we went to Sunday school. You had to be there at 11 o'clock, else you heard it! Farringdon would have been best part of a mile through the Forest and she'd go home afterwards. The dinner was more or less all ready – Grandfather used to look after that. They'd finish dinner about 1 o'clock and Grandfather would get up and he'd go off out – and he was all ready to just saunter on up to the chapel to stoke the fire up, tidy up and that sort of thing. As I say it was about a mile and he'd just go up.

He used to smoke cigars and he was never allowed to smoke indoors. Never. If he wanted to smoke – he had to go in his shed. But Sundays, he'd have his dinner and he'd light up a cigar when he got up the top gate and just saunter on up and take his time. And he was always looking about. He was looking for something different all the time …. he'd take an interest. By the time he got to the chapel he'd finished his cigar. That is why he took his time. Normally he smoked those Mannikin, the small cigars … but as I say, never indoors! And then of course the doors were opened up and about 2 o'clock all the congregation came in and the minister … everyone. The school was the other side of the road. There were a number of us kids, and we had to go to Sunday School. We went to school, and Sundays, we had to go to Sunday school for about hour and a half in the morning and two hours in the afternoon. When we came out of Sunday school, we had to go over the road to the chapel, for the remainder of the service.

After that Grandmother and Granddad, would go back home and have their tea. No doubt, others of the family as well and, of course there was three girls and it didn't take long to get the tea ready and that sort of thing. Then there was nothing else to be done - only feed the pigs and the cattle and milk the cows. Nothing else. Grandmother, I suppose, made the law. If there was some hay ready to be picked up – that stayed there. Nothing – only the essential jobs were done.

In the afternoon, when she got back down the first thing she did was to go up on the hill and feed the chicken. They were half a mile away, across 2 small fields. She used to cook potato peelings, all that sort of thing and mix it up with meal and take it up on the hill. Chicken feed she always called it 'viddles'. 'I got to get the chicken viddles ready.' And why viddles, I don't know, but it was always viddles. Granddad always had some pigs in the sty, and he was always boiling up – and it was 'pig viddles'. Neither of them said pig food; it was pig viddles.

He used to boil up potatoes and different stuff. He used to do a bit of market gardening, and he'd get the green stuff off the turnips or whatever and that all went in the copper. And he had the copper going all the time. He used to go in Southampton – Shirley - once a week, on Saturdays mornings. He used to go by home in the old pony and cart, just before nine o'clock – he'd loaded up with vegetables – turnips, swedes, all sorts he had there, apples and goodness knows what and two or three bags of potatoes. He'd sell them in different shops; then he'd finish up in the Co-op bakery. He used to collect the sweepings and stale bread and anything that was going - for the pigs. I don't think he paid anything for it, mind. They just picked it up. They wanted to get rid of it.

He'd come back and go on up Shirley High Street and pull up outside a tobacconist. Out would come the Tobacconist, 'Same Guv'ner?' He had his regular supply of cigars – every week they used to bring it out – he never got off the cart. They'd bring it out and he paid for it.

I used to go in occasionally with him and I've been in there when he had several boxes of apples left. Perhaps he hadn't sold them. And he'd go back down the sort of street with working people in. A woman might come out, 'Do you want some apples, Missus?' And he'd give them all away. But that was his way of life and I suppose he gained quite a lot of friends that way.

I suppose I started going down there when I was about 10 or 11. And now and again Granddad would say to me, 'Oh, I wants you to lead the horse in the horse hoe.' hoeing the vegetables. 'And don't let her tread on any plants!' He'd be following on along, holding the handles. And if I led the horse out of line a bit, he wouldn't say a word, but I had a clot of dirt or something under my ear! I enjoyed doing it. When we got to the end, turning round, he'd shout 'Keep they traces tight.' And this was it, more or less. That would have been the first time I ever used a horse hoe. I said to him once, 'Can I get up on her?' 'No,' he said. 'You walk in front of her!' He used to shave those lines close. What he used to say was, 'I like to hoe them and make them plants shiver.' He'd horse hoe them a couple of times then he'd go back through and cut them out by hand.

He had a place where he stacked all the vegetables up at the back of the farm buildings. There was a stream ran through – he used to call it the Cutting. It was about three foot wide - rather a fast stream - and nearly always had a fair drop of water in. He started getting his load ready to go to market, or whatever, about Wednesday. He used to tie these bunches of carrots or turnips with a 'with'. How he made them: around the farm there's quite a bit of withy and when the young growth is about 18 or 20 inches high, it is very pliable and he'd go along the hedge and cut about a 100 at a time. He nearly always wore corduroy trousers or, if it wasn't cord twill it was a heavy tweed, a thick tweed. He used to have a leather strap round just below his knee – they were called Yorks. He'd push these withs down through the strap and he'd go along and he'd have 40 or 50 of these strapped in there.

He had quite big hands: they were all lumps and bumps. How he did it, I don't know. He'd pull off a bunch of carrots or turnips, whatever, bunch them up and he'd tie them up with one of those withs, better than you and I could do it with a piece of string. I mean, he'd did it all his life and he knew exactly what to do. I tried many a time, I couldn't do it: I used to break the with. But he didn't he'd just twist them round, turn them round, had an eye there like, poke the end out through, down, round, and he'd bunch them all up. After he'd bunched them all up, he washed the dirt all off in the stream. Everything – carrots, beetroot, turnips, all of them were clean and there was no dirt on them. When they dried out, he'd stack them up and they looked really nice. It was his way of doing it and that was that. On the Saturday he'd go and call in two or three shops – greengrocers, and sell them. Of course, he had one or two favourites, in the Co-op store, he always used to keep one or two back for them.

Granny, she used to go in twice a week. Well, I remember in my younger days she'd go – only went once a week – Fridays. Then I suppose the customers wanted some fresh milk, so then she went Tuesdays and Fridays and that was when Uncle Dan took her in, when he was in his teens. I think Granny went just in this side of Southampton: Freemantle, Shirley, that sort of area. That is where their main customers were. She had an old governess cart: how she stacked it in there, I don't know. All the milk was separated and she made butter - and she also liked to sell the cream. Shiphams meat paste: she used to save those jars for cream. She'd put it in these jars and took them in round the town. And eggs and chickens: she used to take 7 or 8 chickens, perhaps more. Whatever they had to sell, they took.

Buffy Mansbridge: commoner and stock dealer

Len's father, William Mansbridge (always known as Buffy), was a canny but fair businessman. He started up as a small trader after the First World War, and built his business up as a livestock dealer, travelling to markets all over the south of England and into Wales. He also kept horses and carts which he hired out for working on the roads, and to transport the gravel and sand that he supplied for building and manufacture. He was a man of the Forest and knew what it could offer to anyone with the wit and motivation to seize an opportunity when they saw it.

He brought Len, his brother and sisters up in the ways of the Forest. Often he would keep Len off school and tell him that he would learn more at his side than in a classroom. He taught him to ride boldly, how to deal keenly but fairly, what to look out for in an animal, a fellow forester or a trader and how to get by in any company. Above all he taught him to be 'honest, trustworthy and respectful'. He was a hard man in many ways, and Len would never dare to challenge him, but now concedes that he taught him much of what he knows today.

My father was in the Great War - he wasn't with the hostilities - but he did go. I think he was over in France for a bit, and in Belgium. I'm not quite sure. He never spoke much about it. Then, when he came out the army he had to think about making a living and – this is only what I'm told – he went to the fish market in Southampton and got three or four boxes of fish and strapped them on his bike. He went all down round Beaulieu Manor, East End and East Boldre, selling this fish. Also, in those days, most of the cottagers would have a rabbit or two. He used to buy the rabbit skins and, from what I understand, they were about thruppence each - and he used to get about sixpence for them in Southampton.

He did that for quite a while and then he started expanding. The smallholders around the area and the farmers might have a calf they wanted to sell, or a trip of pigs or something like that. There were no cattle haulers. He used to take them to Southampton market and sell them.

If my grandparents wanted a hand with the hay making my father would help, but as far as their trips to Southampton, I don't think he was involved. He was more or less on his own, as you might say. As time went by, Father started with horses and carts on team labour on the roads and gravel carting, sand carting, that sort of thing. He used to haul anything. Later on in the years, he had up to about 12 or 15, but I'm talking about in the early days, when he had about 3 or 4 horse and trucks doing haulage work and he employed men to drive them.

Sometimes he'd be working on the council, repairing the roads or tarring, that sort of thing. Or, if there was a builder wanted a load of sand he'd supply that. At Longdown there were two sandpits and a loom pit[13], then there was a couple of skyony pits. It's grey gravel - very sandy. There's another couple of pits at Fernycroft. The old gravel digger, Mr Smith, lived just below us at Longdown. Father'd either go down to him or the local keeper, and say 'I want 10 yards of gravel, ten yards of sand.' – whatever.

In that sand pit, they always reckoned, there was the finest silver sand in the country. My father had a contract with Pilkington's, the glass people, for 40 or 50 tons a year. They'd order it today and they'd want it tomorrow. And I remember, I was – I hadn't been driving the lorry long. I was about 16 I suppose: 16, 17 perhaps. Anyhow on a Sunday he said to me, 'Oh, be about tomorrow morning. That sand. It's already dug down there. Got to load in on the rail.' He had a small lorry. It was a 30 cwt – that was its capacity - but I used to put 2 ton on it. Monday morning came. He got me out of bed about 6 o'clock and we got started: myself and a chap that worked for Father for several years. There was 10 ton to go. We went down there and loaded up what we thought was about 2 ton and went on with it. Then, we had to chuck it off the lorry onto a truck on Lyndhurst Road station. I got them to put this truck - not where they unloaded the

---

[13] Loam pit, but pronounced 'loom' locally

coal, because we had to chuck it up - but where the horse boxes loaded and unloaded. Then the truck was down there, so we had to chuck it down. It all had to be handled with a shovel. I can tell you, that was probably the hardest day's work I've ever done. We started off just before seven o'clock in the morning, and we never finished up until half past seven at night. We had ten yards (that was five loads) and we never stopped. We ate our sandwiches going from the pit to the station.

When I was about 10 or 11, I remember I went to school, came back, had tea. Father said, 'Oh, I want you to go down Kings Hat. Go down and see Mr Humby. Tell – ask him - could he get me a couple of rabbits.' This would have been Tuesday, and I'd have to go and get them on Wednesday. Two rabbits – one and six[14] a couple. I paid for the rabbits and he give me a ticket – to show that it was paid for. Sometimes I went up to Mr Smith – Bert Smith – up at where John Gulliver is now – to his place[15]. But nearly once a week, I'd go to one or the other place – a couple rabbits was 2 meals.

Hell of a nice bloke - Albert Humby. He was a character - He was a *real* character. I remember one day later on – I was going to Fawley – I had a lorry. I was going to Fawley and I was turning round at Ipley Cross to go across Dibden Bottom. And I could see him on in front pushing his bike. And he had a bag. He used to have an old lady's bike, and he had a bag down in the well of it – pushing on. I stopped and said, 'Do you want a hand, Mr Humby?' 'Oh no, I can manage.' He said. I said, 'Well I can chuck that (it was a bag of rubbish) in the back.' 'No,' he said, 'I can manage. I'm taking this back down Hythe. Somebody dumped it out Ipley. I picked it up and I'm taking back down Hythe where it come from and I'm going to tip it out on their lawn.' That was Albert Humby!

Since I was a boy my father used one of those big cattle carts - some people call them bull-carts - and a pig float. If he had some cattle to go to Salisbury: a couple of heifers and calves he'd put the calves up in the cart and walk on and the heifers would follow. They walked all the way on the

---

[14] Seven and a half pence in today's money
[15] Church Place Cottage

verge - on the grass. But if he had 6 or 7 store cattle or barren cows, he'd drive them over to Redbridge. He had a friend over there had a little field right by the station. He'd put them in this field, go over there early next morning, load them on the rail and quite often go up on the same train to London and walk them on up through the streets up to the market. I helped do that a time or two.

He'd fatten a few pigs - but if someone came along he'd sell them. He couldn't hold anything. And, then he got involved with ponies and, well that was it. He worked his way right up with the ponies. He'd go to Lyndhurst fair and buy them there, and they used to have a couple of pony sales at Brockenhurst market. There was Brockenhurst Monday, Salisbury Tuesday, Southampton Wednesday, Romsey Thursday. If he bought them in a sale like at Brockenhurst he'd send them straight on as they were.

He used to send Forest ponies all over the south of England and sometimes he'd go to Wales. It was Welsh Cob colts he used to buy and bring back. As a boy I used to go with him to different markets: Dunstable, Maidstone, Bishops Stortford, West Malling, Reading and Guildford. Quite often he used Haywards Heath. He'd put most of those going on up towards the Midlands on rail and send them. The auctioneers would take them off and get them into the market for him.

Then he used to go down to Dartmoor and Exmoor buying ponies, at different sales in the autumn. I remember him buying 92 ponies for £96 from Princetown Fair. I was with him like and we loaded them on rail and he sorted them out. He picked out 20 mares and he put them in one truck - sent them back to Beaulieu Road Station. We went over there when they arrived the next day, branded them all and let them out.

Do you know - some of those ponies set straight off for home! I went right on the edge of Dorchester on a farm there and got 3 of them, and I got some more the other side of Ringwood. And there were two, I think it was, that were at a place called Boveridge the other side of Alderholt. In my opinion, those ponies were making their way back to Dartmoor: they were going the right direction. Well, of course, those that went down there, he never kept, he sent them on. He thought if they were going back to Dartmoor, he'd never see them again.

Len as a small boy on a pony

I learnt to ride before I went to school. Father used to take me out, I suppose I'd have been about four. He used to get me up early in the morning before he went off to market or whatever, and go out for a ride. Later on, when we had the riding school, I used the same ride for an hour's ride, but no doubt it took longer then because you go steady.

In those days most Commoners could ride. You learnt yourself; you just had to put the finishing touches on, that's all. Another thing we'd do especially of a Sunday afternoon. If there were any 2 or 3-year-old heifers, we'd go out and get them in and catch one and ride that. And don't you think that didn't want some riding!

As a nipper, Father bought me a donkey and he used to put that in a cart. Weekends, Saturdays, me and a friend used to go out picking up fir cones taking them round the village and selling them for firelighters. Then, we used to use her cleaning out the pens. I remember one time though, she was backed into the yard and I was cleaning a pen out. Father called me to go and give him a hand: he was ringing some pigs. He wanted me to hand the rings to him as he was doing it. He was ringing these old sows: they were going acorning. This particular sow was a bit of a handful. We were sticking the rings in. She went back and broke the rope, went out the door, right underneath the donkey. The donkey just scarpered! She went - cart and all. She went out over the other side of the road from home, carried on up through the wood. Well, today, with the traffic she could have been killed. Then she got stuck between two fir trees and when we got there she was still running with her front legs. Funnily enough the marks are still on those fir trees. I've laughed about that many a time. Today, with the traffic she could have been killed, but she was alright and the cart was alright. If anything happened, you very soon repaired it.

Len mounted on Rodeo

Then, when I was about 10 or 11 my father gave me a 3 year old filly and she was a nice pony. It wasn't very long after that, a Mr McClean came from up Gravesend in Kent - he grazed ponies on the marshes there. He came down to the Forest to buy some Forest mares to put a Thoroughbred horse on. Father had sold him two or three lots and he came down one day when this pony happened to be in the field.

Father said, 'Mr McClean is coming. I can sell that pony.' I said no. Anyhow, he came and he looked at it and liked it. Father said, 'Damned good price. He's offered £3. 10s for it. A damned good price. You can buy another one.' So I sold it. Never had a foal out of it but, of course, I bought another one. That was a good price at the time.

I know one pony I had, I'll never forget him - had him for years. He was a stallion as a matter of fact. His name was Black Jack. Father bought him off old Frank Kitcher: He lived in a thatched place at East Boldre: right down the end of Factory Lane and he was a coalman. He had some good ponies: the old fashioned sort.

Len on Black Jack (right) with Buffy

Outside of the Homestead there was a big tree and a paling fence went along. Father used to tie the ponies on there. He told me that he'd bought this pony, and he was tied on a tree out there. I went out and had a look: he was jet black. He had 'FK' on him: I'll never forget it. Of course, he was just stood there and I wanted to see him move, didn't I! I got a stick and poked it through the rails. He kicked out and knocked one of the palings off: up and knocked some of my teeth out too.

He was a three year old then. Father broke him in: he was hell of a good pony – he'd go until he dropped. I used to go and get ponies anywhere: tie a stallion alongside of him, it would never worry him. Actually he'd keep 'em back. Pony catching: he would stay with them; he was safe. Father would go out pony catching on him and the pony would be beat. I can see Father walking up the road - you're not going to believe this - carrying the saddle and bridle. There were times in the evening, sometimes in the winter, Father would write out a note, and I had to take it to someone for him. It might be old Bob House, Fred Kitcher; all sorts. I'd have to take it down and give it to them like. When I was going home it was dark, that old pony he knew his way up through that Forest like the back of my hand.

I used to put him in a cart and do odd jobs with him. In summertime he was in a horse brake all the time. If there wasn't work at home, a neighbour would come up and borrow him. At times he ran the Forest too; he was a real stallion. When he was out on the Forest, he'd round up his mares and if another stallion got in there, his ears would go back and he'd go straight in and there'd be a fight. You never see that today. Stallions of today have got no masculinity; they go out and sniff one another and that's it. I've seen them stand up and fight one another for an hour or perhaps a couple of hours and then they'd go back and have another go.

I rode him thousands of miles and the only time he ever let me down - I think I must have been about 8 or 9. Father had one or two ponies at Hilltop and he just wanted to go down and have a look round these ponies. We'd been round Hilltop and came back down and there came out onto the road at Rushbush and pulled over on the left hand side. There was a bit of plain and Father said to me, 'Come on, let's have a canter up across there.' So off we went. But the pony put a foot in a rut and tipped upside down. Out I went, didn't I, and I was knocked out. Father sat me up and I eventually came round. I looked up the road and I saw a sight I shall never see again. There was Mrs Humby, she was pushing a pram and she had Bob Humby in it – it was when he was a baby. And she was leading a pony. A woman pushing a pram and leading a pony! That was the first thing I recognised! Anyhow, I come round, got up on the pony and went on again.

When I was a nipper, Father used to buy any amount of ponies down through East Boldre; all the Kitcher family, old 'Lardo' Harvey. When old Bob House was up there, he used to do a lot with the House family - old Granny House – Bob's mother. Sometimes, after I'd been to school, in the evening, he'd send me out to catch a pony - he might have bought 2 or 3 off someone and ….. 'Catch it – And don't come home without it!' So I'd saddle a pony and go down there, and it could have been dark then! I'd ride the pony down and tie one mare on the pony, tie another one on that and just go on! Occasionally, I've come home without it. 'Where's the pony, then?' 'I can't find it.' 'Well you'd better get back out there and look for it!' It wasn't any good saying 'No, I'm not going.' If he told you to do something, you done it! He'd only tell you once. But there it was; I think I'd do it all over again!

I often used to go when Father was selling the ponies. On a Tuesday, I'd be getting ready to go to school, and he'd just leave it till the last minute, 'Oh, you can come with me today. You'll learn more with me.' Of course Tuesday was Salisbury Market and the army would be there. He'd buy one or two or, perhaps, three ex-army horses. He'd say to me, 'Go up round Mr Tills,' (that was the saddler) 'Ask him if you can borrow a saddle and bridle, and bring it back next week.' I went off and got the saddle and bridle and he brought one horse up and put the saddle on and I'd ride one and lead the others back. Many a time I did that. I'd got out of a day's schooling, he always said, 'You'll learn more with me today than you will at school.' – probably I did!

When he used to take these ponies to different markets, he used to halter them. They used to be in a pen or sometimes he'd just halter them in a corner. He used to put the halter over their ears and then pull the rope underneath the jaw like, not pull it up like most people do, just let it over their ears, let it drop down.

Fred Norris Senior outside his shop in Beaulieu

He always took a bundle of halters to market. In those days down at Freddie Norris's, Old Freddie Norris (Old Fred today - his father - he was quite a character), he was a saddler and harness maker, jack-of-all-trades. Father'd buy these halters from him. They were just pony halters and I've never seen them since. They were made of flax - not quite so thick as halters you get today. They lasted for years and they fitted absolutely. He used to take these halters and if he sold a pony he'd give them a halter you see. If I was there he'd say, 'Nipper'll let you have a halter, so you'll have to give him some luck money.' I used to get a shilling perhaps eighteen pence, sometimes two bob. If I remember rightly, those halters were 9 shillings a dozen. It paid me to go!

Then he used to send a load of ponies to Dunster to sell. The next day he'd have some at Maidstone. So he'd come back into London (well it wasn't London, it was Orpington: he had an aunt there and stayed with her), and then go on to Maidstone. I remember one day we were up there, and at the time I couldn't understand it. We'd been to Dunster and sold out. We went back to Waterloo Station. There was a teashop there. We went in there and had some food and a cup of tea. He looked round and said 'Stay in that chair. Don't move,' and he disappeared. When he came back he had a parcel, all done up in newspaper. He'd been out and bought something: that's what went through my mind. He said to me, 'You're not coming to Maidstone with me. I want you to take this parcel straight home. Go back and get on the train and go straight home.'

Of course, I didn't know what he'd gone out and bought. I dare not ask what it was. I got on the train and went back to Southampton, caught the bus out to Hunters Hill and walked home. He'd said to me, 'Take it back and give it to your mother. Tell her to put it in a safe place.' We couldn't work out what it was. I didn't see him till the following morning. He said, 'Did you give that parcel to your mother?' I said, 'Yes, she's got it.' He said, 'I'll go and get it.' He went and got it – it was pound notes! There must have been three or four hundred pounds there. Ponies those days weren't dear. I said 'Why didn't you keep it then?' 'Well,' he said, 'Didn't you have your eyes open? Didn't you see two queer looking chaps stood up all day watching us? Didn't you see them two back in Waterloo Station? They got on the same train as us and they were back in Waterloo Station.' I said, 'Well, yes, I did.' He said, 'I think they was after my money.' But he was one step in front. There were those sort about in those days as well as today: but not so much probably.

Those days there was more cash than there was cheques. He didn't know the people he was selling them to. Actually, with some of the auctioneers, if he sold them privately - sold them before the auction - he'd tell them to go and book it in at the auctioneers' office. He was safeguarded then, and he'd get a cheque in the post. I suppose, as regards cash, he dealt in cash more than anything. Probably bought all these ponies in cash and he sold them in cash and there was no record.

He rented two fields at Marchwood – one where he had the rights, at Byams Park, was about 20 odd acres. I suppose I would have been about 10 or 11. He said to me, 'Get 'em out from there and drive 'em up to

Marchwood station and load 'em.' There was no pound: you just had to hold them there. The funny part of it, I could never work it out: in a railway truck - cattle trucks - you could make them small or bigger - there was a partition, but he always used the small truck. If he had a large truck, of course, it was more expensive, so he had small one. But I mean whether it's large or small it still had to do the same journey. I could never work that one out.

I remember, these particular ponies were going on and the RSPCA inspector that was at Lymington then, he was rather hot. He was trying to stop them going into the truck. He said there was too many. I was only a nipper; I was stood back watching. Father said, 'Come on, get them in there.' This inspector was in front of them and he went in the truck. Father shut the doors up and said, 'He can go on with 'em!'

In those days most animals went by rail, but if Father could save a pound, he would. There was a fellow down at Temple Coombe he used to sell ponies to. This chap would come up by train and Father would meet him a Lyndhurst Road Station. He'd sell him these horses and the next day he'd tell me to chuck a saddle on and ride one and lead one to Temple Coombe: it's some ways the other side of Shaftesbury and it took about 9 hours. I'd come back by rail. To start off with I'd come back to Lyndhurst Road Station, but that meant I had to carry a saddle and bridle home from the station. After that I'd get off the train at Redbridge - that's on the main line - then go out and catch a bus to the top of Hunters Hill, and then I only had to walk from there.

I remember once, he took me to Ringwood Fair – me and the chap that worked for him – Spuzzer – Spuzzer Cook. I was only about 12, I suppose, and I couldn't understand why he took Spuzzer. Anyhow he bought a bunch of heifers. Of course, he had no transport. We had to drive them home! Me and Spuzzer: walked from Ringwood, driving a bunch of heifers.

Another time he bought some ponies and they were in Hythe pound. Father sent me over to get them. One was a stallion - a chestnut - I'll never forget that horse! The pound keeper was an old man. He had a stick – had a job to get about. I told him I'd come for the ponies, paid him and whatever. He said, 'You won't be able to take them.' I said, 'Well I've got to try!' First of all I got a halter on the stallion and he was up in the air. I tied him on the pound and caught the other one and I had a stallion on one side and a mare on the other. I got home. I suppose I'd have been about 12 or 13.

Many a time during the pannage season, when the acorns started to drop, at the weekend, he'd say, 'Now jump on that pony, go out round, and look round the ponies. Just have a look at 'em, see if any got acorn poisoning. You know the symptoms?' I said, 'Well, more or less.' And then, Wednesday, he'd say, 'Don't go to school. Jump on that pony, and if there's one you think got acorns. If you only *think* it's got acorn poisoning, bring it in. Because tomorrow'll be too late. And if there's one of someone else's, in your opinion that got it, when you get home, get in touch with Mr. Forward'[16].

We used to have some laughs and some uncomfortable times. I broke a lot of ponies as a young chap. In those days - well I suppose until about the latter part of the forties - Father used to send a lot on to the pits: pit ponies. He sold them to the person that sold them direct, but there had to be a lot of them and they liked them in chains. He had to put a collar and hames on, then a bridle and lead them on. We had a hook on the hames on the collar and put the chains on them for 2 or 3 days and then they were quiet. They had to be colts or geldings for the pit ponies.

I remember, I wasn't very old, I suppose was 10 or 12 perhaps, and he bought some ponies off Ernie Harris. Ernie kept the Stag Hotel in Lyndhurst and he had Angel Farm. At another time he had The Lonsborough in Lymington - and Dilton Farm. Anyhow, Father bought this particular horse: hell of a nice pony, real old fashioned sort; iron grey. They drove him into a pound at the back of Ashurst Lodge. We got a halter on him. He fought and went up. He was white with lather - through temper more than anything. Finished up, we had to put two halters on him and walked him into Longdown: one walking in front and one behind (he'd come at you, you see). He was tied on for about a fortnight or three weeks, fed on barley straw. In the end he went on to the mines.

One finished up with Ralph Hayward. Father let him have it to break. We

---

[16] Hubert Forward, the agister

called him Satan: he was Satan too! Ralph sent a chap that worked for him to a stable down the road where this horse was, to get a halter on him. This fella opened the door and went in, but he just went round and round the stable: couldn't get near him. It finished up, I got up on a beam and dropped the halter on him from on the beam with a stick. He was a handful. Ralph got round him; he used to ride him out pony catching. He had him for quite a long time.

Another time Father bought two horses off this person. I suppose, I'd have been about 15 or 16. One of them they couldn't do nothing with. It was an Irish horse, just about 15 hands. The most horrible thing you ever want to ride: trotted with its front and cantered with its back. It was terrible: but it would gallop and it could jump. I was out in the field one day, passing the time away, going out to school them - jumps and one thing and another.

I was driving this mare round over the jumps, I saw Father come down the road in the cart - he'd had a wine or two. He would tie a pole up for me to jump, that sort of thing. I mean it wouldn't be loose: if you hit it, you hit it. Between the two fields we'd built up a fence because we had a horse we'd point-to-pointed a time or two: ex-army horse, big raw-boned sort of thing: you couldn't hold him. The fence was on top of a bank and then there was three foot on top of that, gorse and brambles, and there was a rail along a line. He said, 'Put her down over there.' I said, 'No.'

He went off indoors and I thought, well, I'll have a go. So I went down. We used to let them gallop right up through the field like. And she galloped: I can hear her going now! She got up to the fence, and instead of jumping it she jumped on top of the bank and of course these brambles and whatever, she tripped over. We both landed on our feet: she landed on her feet, I landed on mine. He must have looked round and saw what had happened, and he come running out. I said to him, 'Well, she's going to do it next time, so I shall go back down there again.' And she did: she jumped it that time. Looking back, she was an Irish horse and those Irish horses are used to banking, you know, jumped on the banks and all. She saw the bank I suppose: didn't know what to expect. I didn't either!

One day (this was at Maidstone Fair) he'd sent a load of ponies up - 20 odd ponies - the day before and he went up with another person. This other chap's son took me up early in the morning. There were three brothers: one of them drove the car up and I went up with them. We left home about half past four and got up there early, to get the ponies in where they had to go. It was raining: it was just raining cats and dogs! We were wet through; no food nor nothing. About 12 or 1 o'clock, Father came out with three or four others: they'd been in the pub all the time. He looked at me and said, 'Jump in there and pull that chestnut pony in.' I looked at him and he went blue! Well that's how it was: you just done it.

Buffy Mansbridge and Jean Henvest at the Fox and Hounds in Lyndhurst

When I'd just left school, (well, I was coming up to 16, it must have been about 1932 I reckon) there was an abattoir that killed ponies at Totton[17].

---

[17] Hambleys

He bought several ponies throughout the Forest, and one day I had to take 5 ponies down there. When I was down there, there was another lorry load came in – and, some of the best ponies you ever wanted to see. There was, 4 or 5 or 6 red roan. They had a sort of flax mane: they were lovely ponies – to be killed. Well, it did upset me and I never liked going down there. Another time we were loading some ponies to go there - about 20 he'd bought off Frank Shutler. They were all Forest ponies but, there may have been one or two were registered, I don't know, and there was one mare - about a four year old - she was as pretty as paint. It was the same breeding line that did a lot of showing: Burton Slow Lass. I said to Father - I asked him if he'd give it to me. 'No.' he said. The man knows that's coming with the others. And he wouldn't let me have it. He probably had about 5 quid for it, perhaps less.

I used to think he was a hard man but I always felt that was his way of educating me: to be honest, trustworthy and respectful. I believe it. What he said was law. And what he told you to do, you done. From a small age, if someone came to see him and they were talking, I might stay there and listen, but if I opened my mouth, he only had to look at me. That was enough. He always said, 'Be seen and not heard.' His father would be more or less the same as him: very strict and stern. He'd only tell you once. These days if you ask somebody to do something you got to ask them two or three times. If he asked me and I just sat or stood there he'd kick me up the backside and that was that. One thing I will say, he never took his belt off to me, he did it by look or by voice.

His look was enough: he did it the more efficient way. For instance, if I hadn't fed a pony, or hadn't watered a pony or horse, or whatever, when we were having a cooked meal on Sunday, he wouldn't say anything; he'd just pick up my dinner, take it out and put it in the pig swill. He said, 'If that pony goes without his grub, you go without yours.' That was the way he did it. Many a time I've thought he was more than strict. And I was beginning to get fed up at times. As I got older, I realised that was his way of giving me an education.

But I believe he was pretty well liked all over. I remember, much later on, I was out in France one day, in a café having a cup of tea, another fella as well, and I saw these people looking at me. I was beginning to wonder if they were drug dealers: you know you've got to keep your eyes open. Anyhow, one of them come over and said to me 'What part of England do you come from?' Well I told him and he said 'Oh yeah, New Forest eh! – You wouldn't happen to know Buffy Mansbridge?' I said, 'Well, he's my father.' Simple as that.

Ponies and pounds

Before the roads leading from the New Forest were fenced and gridded there were pounds in all the towns and villages on the periphery. When Forest ponies wandered outside the perambulation, seeking the grass and herbs along the roads and into farms, gardens and open spaces, they were rounded up and corralled in the nearest pound, to await collection by their owners. The pound keeper had to see that the animals were fed and watered until their owners came to reclaim them, and made sure that he collected the fines and payments for keep.

For many years through the 1920's, and right up to 1964 when the Forest was fenced, there were running battles over the straying ponies. At the beginning of this period, much of the land through Totton and into Southampton was farmland, and the ponies had traditionally grazed the lanes, sometimes being found as far east as Southampton Common. But as the century progressed much of the area was developed for housing and industry and the ponies were seen as an increasing nuisance.

From his school days in Totton, Len was expected to drive any ponies that he found on the roadsides back into the Forest. And on a number of occasions his father sent him on horseback to pick them up from the local pounds, a job that continued into his adult years. Usually the local agister had been informed that there were animals to be collected. He would identify them and tell the owners of their whereabouts. Len would take all the ponies if he could: it was cheaper that way for the commoners concerned, but you could nearly guarantee that, within a few days, the wily old mares would have found their way back.

I went to school at Totton. Well, I spent 4 years at Longdown School. My own opinion: when Father sent myself and my sisters to private school at Totton the reason for that was he used to keep me home from school to do odd jobs and of course the school attendance officer was always on the warpath. Being a private school, they couldn't do anything about it. I think that was the reason. He never told me.

It only wanted one pony to find a way down into Totton, this time of the year especially, grazing along and they could get into Totton, in a matter of days there would be a bunch of ponies down there and they were impounded. When I went to school there, if there were any ponies about, I'd drive them back out.

I wouldn't know how many ponies I've got out of the pound down there. There was one pound in Brockenford Lane (funnily enough that's where I went to school: the pound was the yard of the building where I went to school). There was a Mr Burt, the pound keeper, a retired person. He lived along not far from the pound. When I was at school the fine was 5 shillings, and then the keep: it was 10 shillings a pony. Mr Burt would say, 'You taking the lot?' I'd say, 'Yeah.' I suppose they had to feed them if there were some left there.

Then there was another pound up at Salisbury Road. I'd be there nearly every week. Actually, there was one erected in the Recreation Ground off Salisbury Road but that didn't work very well. The ponies would get out in the recreation ground and you couldn't catch them in there. That's the reason, I think, it was transferred up the road to what is now the Marchwood Motorway Station. Wally Hodgegood was the pound keeper there. He had a fleet of taxis; I got on with him alright.

Later on, to get the ponies out you had to pay £2, so the consequence was, if there was 5 or 6 ponies in there, I'd take them all out. The agisters would give the owner's name and address to the police, but the pound keeper was employed by the council. You had to pay £2 whether you took one or six. If every owner came and they all had one each, they all had to pay £2. But if I was there with the lorry, I'd take them all out for £2.

The thing was, the ponies did well in Totton. They were on good grazing. There was Rushington Manor, Clay Meadows, the Downs Park Estate - that is this side of Totton. Through Hounsdown, there was Langley House. Then, the other side, there was Testwood Farm, Great Testwood Farm, Hanger Farm. The farmer at Hanger Farm used to impound them himself if they got on his farm.

I remember there one time - a friend of Father's who lived at Minstead had some ponies in there. I was just coming out of school and he was going by and he stopped. 'Chuck your bike up on my truck. I wants you.' We went up to Hanger Farm. The farmyard itself was half a mile or so off the road. They were in the yard. This chap's name was Reg Newman. He was a character in the Forest. He said to me 'I'll go on in front to open the gate on the road. Give me a chance to get down to the road, you open the yard gate and let them out.' Which I did. The farmer was a miserable old devil. He was there, of course. 'Who's going to pay me? Who's going to pay me?' I said, 'I don't know. He told me to drive them out!' That was why he went on in front, wasn't it!

Then there was one at Hythe, one at Fawley, nearly into Calshot. The one at Hythe was right by the Police Station and that was run by an old man, he had a hardware shop: Mr Fry. He used to get nippers to go up the road and drive them down for him. There was a pound at Marchwood as well. I threatened to pull the side of that out one day. Well, I went to collect these ponies and the pound keeper (he was a funny old stick), he couldn't come down and let them out. I said, 'If you don't come, I shall pull the side of the pound out to get them out.' He looked at me and thought I meant it too. I didn't do it: I would have done though!

Going back to Totton pound. There was a piece of ground, about an acre I suppose, which is now a car park, just as you go into Rumbridge Street. It was Rushington Farm. An old man by the name of Andrews kept it. I remember one day I was going to Southampton in the car, the wife was with me. I could see these nippers out in this field driving these ponies around. Then I saw a policeman: I rumbled what was on. He'd got these nippers to drive them out onto the highway so he could impound them. I was straight in there with these nippers, I said, 'Get out of it. Leave those ponies.' It wasn't long before the policeman was in there. 'Look,' I said, 'These kids are driving my ponies about. They're not allowed to do that.' 'Oh,' he said, 'I'm impounding them.' I said, 'Not where they are, you're not. You can't impound these ponies until they're out on that highway. That's why you're driving them out.'

The fact is the police could only impound them from the highway, or if they got in someone's garden or anything like that. Anyhow, we had an argument there. He said, 'I'm arresting you.' I said, 'Go on - arrest me, then.' I went round to the police station. The Sergeant said, 'Well, Mr Mansbridge is right. These ponies have got to be on the highway before you can impound them.' He was a new policeman. The one at Hythe - he used to do the same - but I never caught him out.

Another time I remember Father had a mare and foal shut up in the farmyard down at Newtown Park at Bull Hill. We went down and Father had a friend with him. I had the lorry and he had the car. The farmer said he wanted so much money. I can't remember how much it was now, but it was quite a bit. Father said, 'I'm paying nothing. These ponies are running on the Forest and you should keep your gates shut.' They had an argument and this friend of Father got onto him (Father put him up to it). He said, 'Best thing you can do is take us to court.' In the end he said, 'Load the ponies up and take them on.' The law in the Forest, I was always given it on good authority, is that there has to be a fence and a ditch always kept in good order to keep the ponies out.

Pony racing

Horse and pony racing has been a feature of New Forest life for many years and any event was not complete without at least one point-to-point. Buffy was certainly involved in racing, though when Len was a young boy he was in the business of hiring out ponies for others to ride, and it was he rather than his father, who rode the winners.

Len's riding skills came to the notice of local farmer and businessman, Ted Burry, who owned and trained ponies under rules of the Pony Turf Club. He rode for him as a lad even before he left school and then went on to work regularly as an amateur jockey. He won races across the south and became the owner of a couple of fine racing ponies. He raced against some of the country's top jockeys. At the age of 15 he was set to go on to a professional yard when a serious accident on the Homestead changed his life for ever.

The first time I ever met Ted Burry, I was about 12, I suppose. At the time Father used to buy forest ponies from him, his father and all his family as well as Frank Shutler. Main of them were in the Brockenhurst area. We used to go down there pony catching. Father took me one day. I was riding Black Jack, and there was Ted Burry and Frank Shutler. Ted was on a damn great thoroughbred, used to steeplechase – something like that. Frank Shutler, he was on a big horse – big thoroughbred, and course, out on the open they were fast. And there's me on this little pony: they pulled my leg something wicked!

I had a little hunting crop I'd made. I'd found this stick of ash - about a foot long - the stock. I got a bit of leather bound round to make a little knob at the top. I went down Wilson's the saddler at Totton, and he had some strips of leather for driving whips. I bought one of them for the lash. I think it was one and thruppence. And I thought the world of this. The pony – you could never hit him. If you hit him, he stopped: he'd trot on down the road and all at once he'd stop dead and out you'd go. But I could use this crop on him. They pulled me to bits about the hunting crop.

We met at Aldridge Hill (that's where we drove them in before there were any pounds at Ober or The Weirs). There was a big pound there and we used to drive them from Wilverley down there. Off we went and found the ponies. I kept with them and Ted Burry said, 'That pony goes very well don't he'. I got back to Aldridge Hill, and worked round the ponies and got them in. The others were going on miles: they couldn't turn round on these big thoroughbreds. They came, and I said, 'Where've you been?' Of course, they never pulled my leg no more! But I used to have some fun with them.

Ted Burry trained ponies under the Pony Turf Club rules, and I used to go down and ride for him - well before I left school. He had a racing stables down at Beckett Mayford and I'd go down there at different times. Then, when I left school I went down there about three times a week. I used to ride for them as a jockey - ride their horses out and exercise them.

I used to leave home about half-past four or five o'clock and catch the first train, the mail train, from Lyndhurst Road station here down to Hinton Admiral Station. They used to bring the milk into Hinton Admiral and I'd ride back out with them. I remember one day as if it was only yesterday. I missed the train. So I thought, well I'd better ring up and tell them. So I rang up. He said, 'How'd you get to the station then?' I told him, 'On a bike.' He said, 'Well you'd better ride the bike on down here, then hadn't you!' So, I rode the bike on down there, and I rode the bike down there ever after that. He used to give me 5 shillings a day. The fare on the rail was one and three pence; so I had three and nine pence. When I rode the bike down and back, then I had 5 shillings, didn't I? – I was better off!

Langley Races ca. 1930

We used to go pony racing all over the country. I suppose mainly in Devonshire, but we also went to Wales, and up in Surrey and Essex, to Chertsey, Hungerford. We used to go all over. I won 4 races for Ted Burry in one day down at Wimborne. There was a butcher there had a lorry of horses at the races and he was the only one out of the crowd that backed me. He come up to me and said, 'You can ride that pony if you want to.' So I went and got the one he was pointing at. That was the first time I rode Vim: he was a miniature thoroughbred, about 12.2. I don't mind admitting that first day - they had the local brass band there that started up - he done everything bar turn inside out! He bucked and went up: I was really scared. I rode him a number of times for the butcher, then I gave him £11 for him. That's what I gave him for him.

When I bought him, he'd been turned out and he was poor, but not dog poor. He had a coat like a sheep on him. I got him back home and gave him some grub for a day or two. Then one day I set about and tucked all the hair out of him (his coat was already coming out), and went from there. We used to put him in the 12.2 races, sometimes bigger races. I wouldn't know how many races, I never kept count. We used to go down to Exeter, Lamberts Castle, Weymouth.

Funnily enough, I don't know how he was bred, there was a story that he came out of the mines, but I can't really think that, because he was a miniature thoroughbred, there's no doubt about it. It's the same with some Forest ponies, you get the odd one never grows. As a foal, he only had to get one of those forest flies and he'd turn inside out. He'd kick and go mad. Many a time in the stable he'd kick the roof when he had a forest fly on him. I used to dress him, rub paraffin all over him to keep them off.

One time I remember they had an Injured Jockeys' Fete at Beckhampton. They wanted some ponies for the jockeys for the day and Father had the job of providing them. Fred Darling, the big racehorse trainer - it was on his place that it was held. He was there with Herbert Lalgrave, the racehorse owner and trainer. How it came about: Charlie White used to keep the Fox & Hounds in Lyndhurst and he was Lalgrave's valet at one time[18]. Father was always up at the Fox & Hounds and when Charlie went racing, he went with Father: that's how he got the job.

We took the horses - the ponies rather - up one day and went back the next day and brought them back. Father didn't worry about the outcome: he was being paid to take the ponies up there in any case. There was a hell of a crowd of people there - a fair as well -roundabouts and all that sort of thing. There was an aeroplane there giving rides: they got Father up in this aeroplane.

I had two good ponies. One called Nigger, he was a 13.2 pony: he was a hell of a good pony. The other was Vim. All the top jockeys were there. Freddie Fox, Gordon Richards, Bernard Kerslake, the Smith Brothers. Freddie Fox went up to Father and asked him for a good pony. Father let

---

[18] Herbert Lalgrave lived in Lyndhurst and his mother lived just outside the village, along the Beaulieu Road

him have Nigger, which was the best pony. I was holding Vim and Gordon Richards came up to me - Sir Gordon Richards, I should say. He wanted a good pony. I told him we'd let Freddie Fox have the best one. 'But', I said, 'Have this one. This is a good pony.' So he did. It's a round course, about half a mile round; he had to go around 3 times. I said to him – I've thought about it many a time - me telling Sir Gordon Richards how to ride! Anyhow, I said to him, 'You stick on that Nigger's tail and when you come to that last bend, just keep right on his tail, he's sure to go wide. As soon as there's an opening, go through it.' That's what he done and he won it. He beat Freddie Fox. He jumped off and said, 'That's the greatest little horse ever I've ridden!' He was thrilled to bits. So was I. I've always thought about it though, me - a boy - telling Sir Gordon Richards how to ride a race!

One day I was riding Vim on the Forest. I was after some ponies at Deerleap near the sandpit at Longdown. They went down in this sandpit, but I didn't know the path. He jumped, quite the depth of this room, in there. He landed and kept going!

In those days Father had the stables at Beaulieu Road Hotel. He used to keep 5 horses there, and I used to look after them. One day I was riding Vim over in the afternoon. I had to go back and get some food for 'em. I had a bag of oats and chaff in front of me, and coming back, I was crossing the river at Withycombe, on the corner of Decoy Pond, up over the hill just before the Tinnin Bridge. At the bottom of the hill there was a drainpipe went across. It was just beginning to show, to take the surface water. I felt the pony stumble. I stopped and his hind leg was up in the air: the blood was streaming out. What had happened, he'd have put his foot down through the drain, as he brought it out, he cut those two sinews, there. I managed to get up to Beaulieu Road with him, rung up Father. He came on over and, before he left home, he'd rung up Mr Ripley, the vet (he was the vet at Dibden Purlieu, before Mr Hall Patch. He was the founder of that business). When the vet came, Father sent me out on a horse, but I was only just outside the gate; I wanted to see what was going to happen. I saw they loaded Vim up in the lorry. I went back and asked what they were going to do. They said, they were going to take him to the kennels. I looked at Mr Ripley, I said, 'Can it be healed?' He said, 'Yes, but he'll never be any good'. I said, 'That's all right.' I healed it. As I say, he was never any good after, but I did heal it.

I had two of them, my old pony, Black Jack, and him. During the war I took them and had them put down. I suppose, Jacko he'd have been 28, 30 years old and Vim was getting on. That was the hardest piece of work I ever done. ... They were out in a field down at Mullins Farm in Hythe and Father came there one day. He said, you'd better take those two ponies and have them put down. I said, 'Why, they're alright.' 'Yeah,' he said. 'I know they are. But if you had 'em put down, you'd know where they were. You don't want to see them blown all to pieces with a bomb.' So, that's what I did. But, I know, for a fact, if I had been stopped on the road, and someone had asked me, 'Where are you going?' .... 'Oh, I shouldn't do that.' I'd have turned round and gone back.

Later on, whilst I was a Verderer, we were out on a field meeting looking at seedling firs that needed cutting. Just by where the accident with Vim happened was a bunch of fir trees, they were looking to cut some of them. I wouldn't agree to it. In the end, I said, 'Cut them down in front the hotel, I've had two cows killed there.' They wouldn't listen to me. I suppose there was 18 of us in this meeting. The Head Forester said, 'How about if we take the dead ones out, will you allow that?' I said, 'Well, yes, of course.' They agreed to take several trees out round, but there were two trees right by where this happened. They were going to take them, but I said to the Deputy Surveyor, I'd like to see those two left there (I never said why). They had a bit of a chinwag about it, and in the end he said, 'If Mr Mansbridge wants them left there we'll leave them there.' That was that. I went back there after they'd cut them and they'd cut these two trees. I was really annoyed about that, it was a bit of a memorial, call it what you like.

But going back to the racing, Ted Burry's father had one or two ponies he used to race as well. This was 'Pony Turf Cutting'. They used to race at Portsmouth, Northolt and Weymouth as well as at Lambeth Castle, down in Devon. I remember one time this horse I was riding - 'Grey Rock' - belonged to Ted Burry's father; it was supposed to have won, but it didn't. Ted Burry - he was ill at the time - he wasn't there. I had his father one side of me and his brother the other side of me, sat in the back of the car, from Portsmouth back to Mudeford and I was grilled all the way. As soon as I got back to Mudeford I had to go up and see Ted. When I walked in he had a smile on his face so I thought, that's all right then. 'He didn't win then?' and I said 'No'. 'Oh well' he said 'There'll be another day. You had a rough ride coming home didn't you?' He knew what had happened: it just wasn't good enough.

Actually, I got on really well with Ted Burry. We had some fun; never had a cross word. Very often when he was selling the Forest ponies he'd ring me up, 'Oh I've got some foreigners coming over. Have you got anything you want to sell?' So I'd take them down there. If he didn't sell them he'd give me the petrol money.

I got a fair bit of knowledge there and Frank Shutler – that was Joan Wright's father – one day he said to me, 'You ought to get apprenticed to be a jockey.' He spoke to Father about it. He told him he thought he could get me in a stable. And he got me in the Whitsbury Stables. Stobey the trainer's name was. It was all signed and settled I was going. Then I should be under Jockey Club rules - up the ladder.

And then, Father had an accident with a pony. We had these ponies in the yard, but there was one – a rig. He was a pony about 13.2 and Father was trying to catch him, and he turned round and came at Father with his mouth wide open and bit him through his cheek. It nearly took his eye out: he was in a hell of a state. The chap that worked for Father was there with us. He had to go and sit down, he was so upset. I got hold of Father and took him indoors. Mother was there and she nearly passed out: she had to sit down. So, I went and got a white towel, I put it in some cold water and squeezed it out. I said to Father, 'Hold that there. Don't move it. Just hold it there.' He was conscious - just.

I went on the 'phone to the doctor. Mother was not able to do it. Luckily, the doctor happened to be in; down at Ashurst he lived. Doctor Brierley. 'I shall be there in a few minutes. Get some water, hot water. Get some towels.' The doctor came and cleaned it all up. It was so jagged he couldn't stitch it. So, he bandaged it up and, he came every day then to dress it. After I think it was about 5 days - I can't remember exactly - I think it was about 5 days, tetanus developed and Father couldn't open his mouth or anything. Of course, the doctor was very concerned. He was conscious. He'd get up in the morning and he'd go out in the yard and have a look round, but he couldn't talk to you. The doctor said to me, 'You wanna keep your father interested.' I said to him, 'Well, I go out in the field schooling ponies and...' and he said, 'That would be just right.'

So, I told Father what I was going to do. I was going to take this particular pony out in the field, give him a bit of schooling and I said, 'Why don't you come out there? I'll take a chair out there before. You can sit down.' So that's what happened. Outside the field there was a stile that went into a little orchard. An old man, Old George Pilgrim, used to come every day. He was blind as a bat. But he'd come up every day and sit down on the stile for a couple of hours. He could hear what was going on, but he couldn't see.

One morning I said to Mr Pilgrim, 'I'm going to jump that hedge opposite you.' He said, 'What? On a horse?' I said, 'Yeah'. He said, 'No you won't.' I said, 'Well, I'm going to.' And he said, 'You do it when I'm up there.' I said, 'Well, all right.' So, he came up and sat down. I rode this horse: Kaffa – that was the horse's name. He'd done a bit of show jumping. I'd done it before, never on my own, but Father had made me do it. He said, 'Jump that hedge.' So I pulled round. The pony only had a road – a 4 or 5 foot of verge in front of the hedge. Anyhow, he jumped it. I don't mind telling you, I hit my nose several times. Anyhow, on this particular day, old Mr. Pilgrim was there, and I shouted out to him that I was going to jump it; and afterwards, I heard him say, 'Did you get over all right?'

Anyhow, as I said, Frank Shutler had made arrangements for me, but then this lockjaw or tetanus set in. That changed the story. One morning I'd been out and cleaned out the stables, fed the horses, done whatever. I went in and had my breakfast and I was coming back out as he was coming out of the stable. And I could see ... well, I could see he was worried stiff. I was going to these stables in about 10 days time: it was all arranged for me. I went and met him, and he had a piece of rope in his hand. He hung it on the door. I thought, 'What the hell's he doing with that rope?' He went on up the yard and went indoors. And I got a hold of this rope; I chucked it up in the loft out the way. To be quite honest, it went through my mind, he was going to finish it off; he was going to hang himself. I honestly think that. Then he came out the yard again and something was worrying him. I knew what it was. It was as if he was saying 'You're goin' in about 10 days. Well you can't go, you've got to stay here and look after me.' And I didn't know what to say. I said, 'No I'm not ….. No, I'm going to stay here.' That's what I done.

After I told him, I thought, well, I'll have to go and tell Mr Shutler, and I told Father that's what I was going to do. I got the bike out, rode it down to Burley and I believe I cried all the way down there and all the way back. Anyhow, I got down there, knocked on the door and Mr Shutler came to the door. He said, 'What are you doing here?' 'Well I've got some bad news.' I told him. He knew about Father being attacked with the horse, but he didn't know anything about the tetanus. Anyhow, I told him, and I said, I can't go. And he put his arm round me, and said, 'You've done the right thing.'

I felt so much different after he said that to me but – there it was - I didn't go. So, I've got something to think about now – you might have been a millionaire, you might not. Well, that was it. Looking back on it, the thing was, he had a number of horses there to be looked after, fed and that, shod and whatever. He also had about 10 or 11 cart horses out on hire – team work on the roads - and no-one there could do it. I never dared touch his books before. I looked in them and it hadn't been recorded for weeks: what the different ones had done. So I set to and I wrote it all out, sending bills to the council and that, just hoping it was the right way to do it. It turned out all right in the end, but it was a worrying time. One thing, though, I think it brought me out to live, if you can understand what I'm trying to say.

It went on for some weeks and, thinking back, the doctor knew what he was doing. Father tried to say something but he couldn't. And this is what he was trying to break. But, one day I was jumping a pony out there and he was sat down. He pointed to the 5 bar gate. I said, 'No, he won't do that.' I went on round the field and I thought, I don't know, I'll have a go. He jumped over – he jumped over it like a cat. I said, 'How was that?' You could see his face change – and he sort of pointed to me to do it again. I said, 'No. I know he can do it. It's good enough for me. I'm not going to take the chance. If he jumps again and knocks it down it'll upset the pony and it'll upset me.' So, I never did it … but I think that did Father more good than me. But it's … anyhow … it's one of those things.

Mullins Farm and Wartime

Shortly after Len's marriage to Joyce, a local girl, they moved into Mullins Farm at Hythe which he ran for his father. Their three children, Sheila, Marion and Lennie, were all born at during the time they spent at Mullins. Len built the farm up from the derelict condition in which it was taken on. By the time of the Second World War he had a milking herd and was rearing pigs, as well as growing crops on the arable land to feed his livestock and bring up a growing family.

They watched the War being played out on both sides of Southampton Water, and sometimes it came horribly close to them. Len was made animal warden for the area, seeing that dead and injured domestic animals were disposed of humanely and quickly; and carried on his farming as best he could under the threat of bombing. But, even before the end of hostilities, Len had a more immediate threat to cope with: in 1944 his farm was caught up in an outbreak of foot and mouth disease, and he watched as his entire dairy herd was destroyed and buried on the farm.

In 1939 I married Joyce Ransom. I knew her because I only lived a couple of miles down the road. Her parents kept the pub at Hounsdown, Totton. In those days it was The New Inn. Joyce's father had a few ponies. When we were married, he gave us a pony. They originated from old Harry Marchant's breed. He had the Waterloo Arms at Lyndhurst. When he died they were all sold out.

Then, just before the war, we went to Mullins Farm at Hythe. I was running it for Father. When we went there, it was more or less derelict. How it came about: there was an estate of 3 farms sold and Father went to the sale to buy. It went beyond his reach. He went and spoke to the person that had bought it, and he agreed to rent it. Mullins was sold for I think £3,070. Claypits Farm was just a little bit more. Home Farm - down at Dibden - that made I think £4,000. I can't really remember, but as regards today's prices it was nothing.

There was an old man there, a Mr Curtis and he packed up. But the year we went in they had 11 sacks off 15 acres of wheat. That was just under a sack to an acre. There was 76 acres in all and there would have been about 35 or 40 acres that hadn't been ploughed for years, they were arable but they were just let go: thistles, docks and whatever. It wasn't grazed either really, because he just had a few cows. I ploughed it all with horses, main of it I suppose with a pair of Forest ponies. Sometimes I had a carthorse, but not very often.

I had learnt to plough and that when the old farmer on a little farm in the village died and the son - he was too tired to get out of his own way. Father used to rent about 9 acres I suppose, and used to grow taters, kale, different things. You learn as you go. In those days, if you wanted some seed - oats or wheat – you'd go down to see old Freddie Norris; he'd help you. He'd let you have them and pay when you like or when you could. You can do anything if you make your mind up to do it. I don't mind admitting - ploughing, once you got the plough set right - it's no bother you just go up and down the field, up and down the field, but if you've got it just an inch out of line, you're out all the time.

I also had a donkey which I used for horse hoeing: he was brilliant. He'd go up and down those lines. Actually this particular donkey came from Lord Montagu. When he was a youngster, the present Lord Montagu's nanny took him out in the donkey cart. Then I believe they used the donkey around the Palace House: round the garden that sort of thing, doing odd jobs. I bought him off Fred Richards, he was a gardener there, he lived down at Gatewood near Blackfield. He got in touch with me, said he wanted to sell this donkey. I went down there one evening, bought the donkey and a working cart, and a driving-out Governess cart. It was a square one; it was good. I bought it all, I was just leaving, and he came out, 'Oh,' he said, 'Come here a minute. There's four chairs here I'll sell you.' I said 'I don't want none.' Anyhow I went back and bought these chairs. They were really nice chairs. As a matter of fact, we've still got them today. I put the chairs up in the cart that had nothing in it, and my bike on top of that, and led the donkey home, in one cart and pulling the other one.

There are jobs on a farm you can do in the daylight but you can't do in the dark. In the winter, very often I milked the cows after tea: the only thing I had was a hurricane lamp. I had to carry milk from the cow pen down to the dairy: it would be 70 or 80 yards, I suppose. When the war started, of course, I wasn't allowed to carry a naked light outside. As a matter of fact, the first doodlebug that came down in the area came down on the farm. We had one of these Morrison shelters - the iron ones[19]. We had kids then and they were in that. We heard it coming. Our house was an old

---

[19] A heavy metal table that doubled as a shelter where families, especially children, often slept.

house: the dust that came down - you couldn't see across the room. It was amazing where it came from. Anyhow, in minutes the police from Hythe were up there wanting to know where it landed. I said, 'Well, I don't know. Out near Dibden Purlieu, as much as anything.'

Dibden Church, damaged by bombing

We still didn't know until the next morning. It came down in a field of wheat which it was right up and just about to turn. It cleared everything: there wasn't anything at all left. The funny part of it was, the cows were lying down just over the hedge from where it went down, and none of them had a scratch on them. The blast must have gone out up over them because there were windows and doors blown out in Southampton from it.

I know a number of times I was up on the top during the night: bombs came down in Purlieu or in the area, and a time or two the blast knocked me down. Well there was lot worse off than me. Southampton was more or less flattened. From our backdoor we could look right over into Southampton and watch the bombs come down and there were fires all over the place: something I don't want to see again.

War damage in Winterton Terrace, Dibden

During the war I collected pig swill from Marchwood Army Camp and Lime Kiln Camp (that was an ack-ack site[20] right on the edge of the Forest, the end of Lime Kiln Lane). My father-in-law had been collecting it but he got fed up with it and I took it on. I carried on for several years until it was beginning to dwindle and was hardly worth collecting. Then, in 1944, I had Foot and Mouth on the farm and they wouldn't let me go in the camp. A local farmer took it on, but he didn't last long; it just dwindled out.

I took the kids to school on the way. When I got down the Camp, I'd go in the cookhouse and get a couple of pieces of bread and a couple or three pieces of bacon and have a bacon sandwich; that was my breakfast. I

---

[20] Anti-aircraft gun site

remember one day they started to shoot the camp up with machine guns. I was outside the cookhouse. Of course, they told me to go in, I said, 'No I can't do that, I can't leave the pony.' I stood outside holding the pony, sort of calming him down, cause there was a lot of activity going on. I stayed there with him and thought, well if he goes, I goes. That was the worst experience I had really.

During the war I was animal (ARP) warden. I don't know how I came by the job, but I've got a feeling a local butcher put his spoke in (he was a friend of mine) and I got on quite well with the Sergeant of Police down there. He used to keep a few pigs and I would take them to the bacon factory for him when he had them ready (there was a bacon factory at Downton and another one at Eastleigh), that sort of thing. I think that's what happened: one of them put me up for it.

I had to dispose of any animals which were injured or killed. It was mostly farm animals but there were private riding horses or ponies. Some of them were not a very pleasant sight. I made arrangements with two different knackermen. I used them alternately: if there was a lot they wouldn't want to cope with it, so I spread it out. Anything alive had to go to the slaughterhouse. If they had a broken leg, they were able to travel, so they went to the slaughterhouse. Well, there weren't all that many but there were too many, if you understand.

The Police Sergeant got me on a different job one Sunday morning, though. He sent a policeman up: could I go to Penerley with the lorry; there was a smashed car he wanted me to pick up. He told me when I had to be there to meet him. I got there, loaded the car up, it was only a little coupe thing. 'Oh,' he said, 'Don't go yet.' They brought a body out, didn't they! 'Put the body up as well,' he said. I dropped that off at the hospital. It was an accident: he ran out of road, went down over in that deep ditch. He was killed. In those days you didn't worry about time, if there was something to be done, you did it.

I did milk a dairy of cows at Mullins, building them up. Then, in '44 there was Foot and Mouth down the road, a mile down the road, in pigs. There was another case at Blackfield. I got up one morning and milked the cows. I had about 18 or 20 that I hand milked. I milked them and went back and put them down the field. Then I went back indoors and had breakfast before I went back up the yard and fed the pigs. Two of the pigs didn't get up to feed. I almost knew they had Foot and Mouth disease. I got on the phone to the vet, Mr Ripley, and he came straight down. We caught the pigs before he came: they were on their knees. I could see something on their feet, but anyhow the vet was coming.

I caught them again, he examined them and told me exactly what it was. 'Sorry Leonard. You've got Foot and Mouth Disease.' As I say, I almost knew it. Within about an hour and a half, the Ministry was there and no one was allowed in or out the farm gate. Police on the gate. Then a digger came in that day. Next morning the slaughter men were there. They slaughtered everything, all the cows and the youngstock, everything. The digger dug a big hole out in the field. They were all buried in quick lime out in the field. It was all over in about 25 or 26 hours. The interesting part of it now, looking back, when these animals were buried, the only water we had was well water. The well wouldn't have been 150 yards - between 150 and 200 yards - away from where those animals were buried, and it was downhill. We didn't even think about it, and I don't suppose anyone else did.

We were paid compensation, but I don't mind telling you, when those cows were slaughtered - and the youngstock - I couldn't stay there. I was milking the cows twice a day. They were all different characters; they all had names. If they were out in the field and I called one by name they looked round at me. No, I don't want to see it again.

When we were at Mullins, a grey pony I had – Misty - one of the best ponies I ever had. He was a jack of all trades: he used to go out pony catching, go and get the kale in for the cows. I used to use him for whatever I needed to do. I had some ponies on Balmer Lawn and some more up Markway. I'd catch a pony and tie him on, and he was only 12.2.

We had a Reading Cart, that's one of the high ones - sort of market cart: you'd just get the reins, click, and away he'd go. We went to a friend's wedding - a Commoners' wedding – Ralph Hayward. The wedding reception was at Ipers Bridge. There was the wife, myself, Sheila (she would have been about four), and Marion - she was still in arms. Anyhow, we were going home. We left there about 11 o'clock at night, went to Hilltop and then back to Dibden Purlieu.

We'd just turned the corner and got on the Dibden Purlieu road – we'd gone about 200 yards or so (there was a barrage balloon site just there). All of a sudden there was sort of a 'Weech!' and the cart tipped upside down. The wheel had broken off: the axle broke. I was over on the right hand side. I went straight out over the wife and the two kiddies. What flashed through my mind was I could imagine this pony going up the road pulling the cart with my wife and children in it. I went straight to his head and - do you know what - that pony never moved. Funnily enough some of these Air Force chaps came out the hut and helped me. We got them out the cart and put Sheila on the pony and Joyce carried Marion home. I went back a day or two afterwards and got the cart, the axle had broken right off by the cart. I suppose it could have been like it for quite a while.

Len holding Misty, with Lennie and a friend in the cart

Then I used to drive Misty on August Bank holiday, down to Burley Show. Me, the wife and kids. When I got there, in those days you used to have a gymkhana: musical chairs, bending and all that. I used to take a saddle with me. He'd go in the musical chairs and bending. Musical chairs: he just loved it. As soon as that music stopped his ears would go back: he was mustard. I won 2 or 3 events like that. I remember Sir Berkley Piggott was controlling the music in the caravan, I had to go by him each time. He said, 'I'm going to get you in a minute!' but this particular time he didn't. We used to have some fun!

I remember one year - must have been about '44 or '45[21] - I put him in the driven class. I didn't get first prize, but I had second. There was - there still is today - a special cup for best pony driven to the show. I was awarded that, but chap that won the driven class objected. I think it must have been the next day he objected to it, because he won the driven class and he said he should have had that prize too. Anyhow, there was a special meeting about this at The Grand Hotel at Lyndhurst one evening. I had to go to it. Jack Ings was the judge and O.T. Price was there out of interest. Jack Ings knew I came from Hythe[22] to the show. That was about near enough 12 miles, and the other one came just a half mile down the road. He'd driven to the show, yes, but it was no distance, and that's when Jack Ings stood his ground. He said, I awarded it to the best pony and in my opinion that was the best pony because he came about 12 miles. I always remember when I was coming out, O.T. Price tapped me on the shoulder (Jack Ings was with him) and he said, 'Now you always remember this: the judge's decision is final.' Which it is!

But, it's funny: an animal you like, you get on well with. If you don't like it, you can't get on with it at all, whether it's riding, driving or whatever. When I used to plough with horses, there were times I had a horse and I didn't like it, and something was always going wrong. At Mullins I had two Forest ponies I ploughed with, cut the grass, and so on. One was about 13.2, the other one was slightly over. The 13.2 one was a strong forest pony: Brown and Harrison, the milk dairy in Southampton, had bought him for one of their milk carts.

In those days, they always docked horses: I think that's what upset him. And he was upset: he smashed up a float. I happened to be in a pub one

---

[21] Len is mistaken here. The cup he won records the date as 1952.
[22] On this occasion he would have come from Ashurst

day when someone was talking out of turn. I heard what they were saying: they were talking about buying this horse. I thought, 'Well you'll have to be up early in the morning to get there.' Early next morning, I said to Father, 'I want to take the lorry. I've got a little job I want to do.' He said, 'Where are you going?' I said, 'When I come back I'll tell you.' I went into Brown and Harrison's office to see the manager. He wasn't there, but the man told me where he was. He said, 'Be careful with that horse.'

I went up to the stable yard and told the manager and groom I'd come to have a look at this horse. He told me where he was, he said, 'Don't go in there with him: he'll kill you.' I knew the animal. I went in this loose box where he was, I spoke to him. He was absolutely scared to death. I went back to the office, asked them what they wanted for him. He said £10. I said, 'No that's a lot too much money, for a horse like that. You don't know what's going to happen.' In the end I gave £6 for him.

I went back up and told the chap I'd come to pick him up. I said, 'I'm going to do this myself. I don't want any help at all.' I backed up to the stable door, put some doors up either side, went and let him out. He went straight up in the lorry: I shut the tailboard up. The only problem was when I got home! Anyhow, I got a halter on him, put another rope on and threaded it through a ring in the stable and dropped the tailboard. Out he darted, straight in the stable. I pulled the rope up and I had him. If he'd got out in the field, I don't know where he'd have gone to. First of all, I made a fuss of him for several days so that he got my confidence and I could get his. Then I went out and lunged him a time or two.

A few days later I wanted to do some harrowing, so I went and got him. I had this old mare, I'd already hitched her on the harrows, and went and got him, hitched him on, away he bounded. I didn't know what was going to happen. He was pulling this other horse around. In the end I had about an hour like that. Eventually I took the other horse off, and let this one go on his own. Finished up, he was white with lather; he was only too pleased to stop. I worked him for a few days like that on the harrows mainly: then I got him on the plough.

In the end he came to it. Same as I say, he was frightened. You dare not touch his hindquarters. It was docking him that done it, there's no doubt whatsoever. He would have been about 4 years old when he was docked.

He was a strong pony like. I suppose it was done under anaesthetic, but there must have been a certain amount of feeling there somewhere. After his tail was off, he knew it, when the life came back into it. Funnily enough, I've got one of the old dockers now. It's like a nutcracker, but there's a blade in it, you put it up over and pull it down over, just like that.

I only ever saw one docked, that was one of Father's. The vet came out and done it, I wasn't very old then, he sort of held the tail over a wall and done it that way. That's the only one I've ever seen docked. I think in some places they still do it. Myself, I don't think it smartens them up at all, yet years ago nearly all the horses were docked, hunters and all.

Tippett, who lived where Raymond Bennett lives now: it was him that sold it to the dairy. I got to hear the history about it, that they docked it. I remember one day (in those days perhaps of a Sunday evening, we'd drive up to the wife's home), we had a governess cart. I jumped up in the trap. As I was straightening up I just touched him on his backside with the reins. I could see it coming! He went berserk! Luckily I knew what to do - I spoke to him and pulled him out of it. You had to be careful when you were driving him.

I had that horse, I suppose three years. Ted Burry rang me up one day. He said, 'A friend of mine wants a cob to work on this market garden. A good Forest pony would do.' I said, 'Well I've got one'. He brought this man along. He was an old man - about 74 or 75 - something like that. I thought, 'I can't sell this horse to him.'

When he first came, he didn't buy him, but he came back a few days afterwards with his son-in-law. He said he wanted to buy this horse. I said, 'I don't think I can sell him to you. I think he'll be too much for you at your age.' He kept on. He was there all one afternoon. In the end, I said to him, 'Well now, look. I'll sell him to you providing you do what I ask you to do.' He said, 'What's that?' I said, 'Never give him any oats. Just give him bran, no oats, because if you do he'll be too much for you.' Anyhow I sold it to him; took it down New Milton for him.

If I should happen to be that way I'd call in: it was always on my mind. I used to call in there and see how he was going on. I called in there one day to see if everything was all right. He said, 'Well, I done what you told me not to do. I know now!' Well I suppose he had it for years. He's dead now.

Ashurst Lodge

In 1947 the lease on Mullins Farm was terminated and Len had to find another place to farm and live. He chanced on the information that Ashurst Lodge was empty and might be for rent. With the help of a friendly local estate agent, Len managed to secure the land and buildings, and so set himself up as an independent farmer for the first time. At first the family lived in an old gardener's hut by the railway line but, after the lease had been bought by Hampshire County Council, his request for a house was granted and he moved into it in 1963.

He used the old commoner skills that he had learned as a boy, keeping pigs and cattle and harvesting anything that the Forest offered to make a living. He had brought two in-calf heifers with him from Mullins, and they formed the basis of his new dairy herd. By the 1960's he was milking 20 cows when his herd was struck by a mysterious sickness which killed several of them and led to the cancellation of his milk contract. Undaunted by the catastrophe and ever looking for a new opportunity, Len then changed to suckler cows and started selling ponies into the newly opened market for export to Europe.

We were under notice to get out of the farm at Mullins in 1947. One of the syndicate that owned the farm was getting married and he wanted the farmhouse. We had to get out by September.

I was looking for a smallholding: somewhere to live as far as that goes. I went on a number of day's outings looking and couldn't find anything. Then, one day there was a little farm sale up at Foxhills Farm, Twiggs Lane, Marchwood. I jumped on a bike and went up there. Mr Hewitt was the auctioneer. I heard from someone at the sale that Ashurst Lodge was empty. I'd known Ashurst Lodge all my life. I went up to Mr Hewitt and said to him, 'I hear Ashurst Lodge is empty. Do you think it's any good me trying to get it?' 'Yes,' he said, 'It is. We've got it on our books. Don't stay here, you go up there. There's a caretaker there. Go up now, get the address of the owner, and write to them.'

He told me then, 'Now you just ask if they'd let the summer grazing and the buildings. Make sure you put the buildings down because if you can get the buildings you've got your foot in.' That's what I did. I went up there and I got three addresses: one in Jamaica, one at Lingfield in Sussex and one in Scotland, I wrote to them in Lingfield and had a letter back saying they would let it; would I offer a rent. I offered a rent and sent the letter back. They accepted. I put a cheque in the post (it was about all I had) and that was that.

Mr Hewitt warned me, 'Now, don't you say a word to no one - and I mean no one!' That was that. I never said a word even to Father. I took Ashurst Lodge in April '47, but I had to get out of Mullins in September.

During the summer at Mullins, I got on and did all the work, haymaking, harvesting, whatever. I had to make sure Mullins was done: I was doing it for Father. As soon as I'd finished cutting the grass and doing the haymaking at Mullins, I took the mower and one of the ponies up to Ashurst Lodge, and left it there. I went up a day or two afterwards, and cut one field there with the pony through the night: it was moonlight. One or two of my wife's family helped me. We picked up loose in those days. We had to chuck it up loose in a pair of trucks and chuck it off in the barn.

When we actually moved, I had the old lorry. We did it by ourselves: took all our furniture up to Ashurst Lodge. There was no house there so we put it all in the cow pen. We lived with Joyce's parents in Hounsdown for about 3 or 4 months, probably a bit more. I was milking 3 or 4 cows then.

The owner of the Lodge and her husband came in one day: they were called Crum Ewing. I'd known her years previously, because she used to borrow a pony from Father for her kids. He was quite friendly with the groom there in those days and I used to take the pony up to Ashurst Lodge for her children.

We never met again until that day. She said 'I remember you bringing the pony up here.' Anyhow, she asked me how I was getting on. When they came I was just getting the cows in to milk in the afternoon. She said, 'Oh, you're milking cows. Really you ought to be living here then didn't you?' I said, 'Well it would be very nice.' 'Alright,' she said, 'there's a bungalow at lower garden - down across the field. One of the gardeners lived in there.' It was an old ex-army hut from the Great War. The electricity cable was broken. She said 'I'll get that repaired and you can go down there.' And that's what happened.

They saw that I had some pigs as well. Her husband, 'Oh,' he said, 'You don't know where I can get some home-cured bacon do you? I said, 'Yeah, I've got some.' So I went down the house and cut off a piece of bacon.

Later on[23] the lease on the property was put up for sale by auction. I think it was 76 acres, the big house and three cottages, and there was 36 years to run. The asking price was £4,500. Unbelievable, isn't it? I never asked questions because I thought, I'm only on a shoe-string. Anyhow, I went to the sale. It was up at what was the Grand Hotel at Lyndhurst, there was only two of us there, myself and another fellow. I only went to see who bought it, so that I could go and introduce myself and get the first one in. But it wasn't sold, so things went on as usual for 2 or 3 months, maybe more. Then I had a letter from Mr Hewitt making an appointment to see me. I was a little bit concerned. I thought, 'He's sold it and we got to get out' Anyhow, he came along and he said to me, 'I expect you wonder why I want to see you.' I said, 'Yes, I do.' He said, 'I want to sell you the place.' I said, 'You must be joking!' He said, 'No, I'm not. We want to get it off our books.' Well, the full story was that the reserve at the sale was £4,500 for 36 years leasehold. We talked about it. I said, 'I've got no money.' - which I didn't. I had a few cows, a few ponies, a few pigs, but it was no good going to a bank: in those days you couldn't get an overdraft or anything else.

He kept on and said, well make me an offer. I thought about it. Well: £1,000 - I might scrape that up, a few pigs and ponies, whatever. I said, 'All I could go to would be £1,000. He said, 'If you jump once more you could have it.' I've always said, if I could have gone to £2,000, I'd of had it. Well, consequence was, I didn't have the money, and that was that. We parted good friends. About 6 or 8 months after, Hampshire County Council gave £8,500 for it. I've always said, they were sniffing about the place, and he was trying to put it my way. But being the person he was, he couldn't tell me.

The American Troops, had been in the big house in the war. Of course that wanted a lot of work done on it internally. The cottages were let. Well, I say they were let: the caretaker lived in one (I don't know, but I think

---

[23] The lease on Home Farm was varied in 1952, and this attempted sale presumably happened some time before the variation. From the fact that the remaining lease was 36 years, it was probably in 1949.

rent-free). The two other cottages probably had to pay rent. They were all railway porters, so I think one told the other, when there was one empty. There it was. So, then I paid rent to Hampshire County Council. I got on quite well and the Council Land Agent helped me a lot.

One Monday morning, the wife got onto me about it being damp in the gardener's hut, which it was. It was only a wooden place. I was walking up across the field and I saw the car coming in. I thought: that's the County Council Land Agent. What's he want? I got up to the path and the gate they were stopped at. I said, 'Good Mornin', Sir. What's your trouble today?' 'Oh.' he said, 'We only dropped in to see if there's anything you wanted.' I said, 'Yes there is. I wants a new house.'

He looked round at his secretary, 'Put that down, will you. Put it down on the pad.' About a fortnight, 3 weeks afterwards I had a letter from them to say the Forestry Commission had agreed to put me up a new house. I got a new house. They increased the rent, but not a lot. [24]

The old house is still there: it's rather dilapidated mind. How it was: we moved up into the new house. I asked the agent, did I have to pull the old house down, he said, 'I suppose you should do.' I said, 'But can I keep it for hay and straw.' He gave me permission to leave it there to put the hay in. Not that I had anything in the back of my mind, I wasn't bright enough then I suppose, about getting planning permission and putting another one up.

Some time after[25], the Forestry Commission Deputy Surveyor and the Land Agent came to see me and asked me what I wanted to do. The Deputy Surveyor said, 'Do you want to stay here?' I said, 'Yes, of course I do.' He said, 'All right. You'll be paying us rent instead of the County Council. We'll draw you up an agreement and we'll go from there.' The rent was the same. It went on about a month - six weeks - then I had a letter from them to say that Head Office had told them to put the place

---

[24] The house was built by Hampshire County Council in 1963.

[25] It isn't clear when this happened or whether Len actually paid rent directly to the Forestry Commission at the end of the lease. Forestry Commission documents indicate that Hampshire County Council gave Len notice to quit in 1984, prior to the end of the lease in January 1985. This was to allow the Forestry Commission vacant possession of the Farm, which was then offered to Len to buy as the sitting tenant.

Marion feeding an orphan foal outside the Gardeners' Hut

on the market. They had already sold the big house and 13 acres and the cottages, so that all they had left was the farm.

Then when I bought it off the Forestry, the agent was looking round making notes on everything, because I left the buying to him. I asked him about the old house. 'You leave that there. You might get planning permission one day.' I think that might come off one day. There's water there you see and electricity. You'd want some new poles down across there. There's a cesspit there as well. What I have thought, Andrew my grandson - I think he'd like to be there. I thought about it: these days you can buy these wooden chalets. So it's still there.

When I started at Ashurst, I used to get pig potatoes from Toogoods in Southampton. I was in there one day, and the head gardener came around. He come up to me and said, 'You comes from the Forest don't you?' I said, 'Yeah.' He said, 'Can you get any sphagnum moss out there?' He explained, but I knew more or less what he meant. 'Yeah,' I said 'There's plenty out there.' 'Well see if you can get some and I'll buy it off you.' I went down to the local keeper, Bert Smith, and told him I wanted sphagnum moss; could

I get it? 'Yeah,' he said. 'It's a shilling a bushel.' I said, 'Well could I have a bushel for a sample?' He said, 'If you want a sample go and get some.' So I went and got a potato sackful and took it in there next week. 'Yeah, that was all right.' he said to me. 'How much is it?' I said, 'I wouldn't know. I've not done anything like this before.' He said, 'Well, I can give you 10 shillings a bag.' I thought, well that's money for old rope. He said, 'I want 40 bags now.' So I got 40 bags.

I pulled it out by hand. There are mounds, and then again it grew in the bogs. It was wet but there was more. It went on from there. A few weeks afterwards, they wrote and asked me: they wanted 50 or 60 bags for Chelsea Flower Show. I suppose they would have had anything up to 200 bags a year. Also, I used to go out Ferney Croft and get leaf mould (I'd get a ticket from Albert Humby). If they wanted flower stakes, I'd get them off my uncle who was working in the copses like. It went on for a number of years till Toogoods closed down. That's how I got a few quid together.

When we left Mullins, I had two in-calf heifers. We had a sale at Mullins, but I didn't sell them. Actually, it was in the back of my mind: I'd keep these two and start a dairy some time. When I went to Ashurst Lodge I had £6 in the bank. These two cows calved: heifer calves. I made arrangements with the Milk Marketing Board and I sold the milk. I used to push the milk down to the end of the road: it's just over a mile. I went on a bike, one churn one side, one the other. I went to Salisbury - only a week or two afterwards - and bought an old Guernsey cow for £5. There wasn't much left in the bank. We waited for the milk cheque.

I gradually built the herd up. When I had the money I'd buy a cow, and I did have one or two heifers coming on. I got up to, I should think, 18 or 20 and the trouble was, in the cow pen, I could only stand four: I had to milk in relays. So, I wrote to them one day asking if they could turn the top barn into a cow pen. The walls of the old barn had collapsed and there was only the roof that was intact. The agent came and saw me and I told him what I wanted. He said, 'All right we can do that. I shall have to increase your rent.' I said, 'All right.' Then I did say to him, 'The walls is your problem isn't it.' 'Oh yes,' he said, 'But it's all alright.'

Then about 6 or 7 councillors came to inspect it before they would do anything, which was fair enough. There was one was an ex-farmer. The agent knew what I wanted. 'We'll have to increase the rent,' he kept on saying it, and this farmer kept trying to put words in my mouth. I couldn't grasp what he was trying to do. Then it came across me - I said, 'You've got to do the walls.' 'Oh yes,' he said, 'We've got to make them sound - and the roof.' I said, 'What about if I do the inside, like, put the mangers in and make the stalls, the concrete and all that.' The farmer said, 'That's what I've been wanting you to say!' They couldn't put the rent up: the walls and roof they had to do. You live and learn.

'Course, I was in. So, that's what happened. I could milk another 10 in there, so that was so much better. I got up to about 18 or 20, and then disaster struck. I lost 2 or 3 cows. They died. I couldn't make out what was wrong. When George Gould, the vet, came and examined them, he said he thought it was poison. We went out and walked that river up and down, up and down, see if there was anything he thought might have poisoned them. I was out there with him one day and we walked right up the river to the sewer beds. These were the old sewer beds, not the sewerage beds today, the old sewer beds; the overflow ran into a ditch and down into the Beaulieu River. We discovered that this sewerage plant had collapsed and the raw sewage was going down into the river. He took a sample and that was the cause: these cows had salmonella. It finished up I lost five cows and three heifers, I think it was. One, I'd only had her just about a month. I gave a fair bit of money for her. It was a heifer, nice heifer. New Forest Council, County Council, the Verderers and the Forestry Commission, they didn't want to know – none of them wanted to know. There was only one person came and inspected it: that was old Archie Cleveland. At the time he was the Chairman of the Commoners' Defence. And he was the only one that came and looked at it – to my knowledge. Down there at Sandhole you can walk through that river: if you scuffed your feet on the river bed, it'd come up like a lot of ink. It killed all the fish and that, but I didn't get a penny of compensation.

By this time the milk I sent out was coming back and it got to a stage where there was more milk came back than I sent. It finished up the Milk Marketing Board stopped the contract. Well, I thought, the milking's gone, I got to do something. I had to get rid of the milking herd and do something. As it happened, eighteen months, two years previous – I'd wanted a bull. When I started the dairy I used insemination, but I got no luck at all. The consequence was: if the cows didn't calve, I didn't have any milk. So I went to Salisbury one day, to the bull sale. I didn't buy anything in the auction. I was about to come home when there was a person from Cumbria, he used to bring eight or ten bulls - Shorthorns, Galloways, Herefords - to the bull sale. He'd more or less sold out but he had one left: it was a Galloway and it was 2 years old. I was looking at it and I plucked up courage to ask – to see what he wanted for it. He said, 'I was hoping to make £100 on him.' I said, 'Oh, we just as well forget it.' But he wouldn't let me go: 'How much would you give me for it?' 'Well,' I said, 'Nothing like that; about 50, 60 quid.' Of course, if he took it home, that was costing him money so, it finished up, I gave £63 for it. So, when this happened, I had the suckler herd half made. I had one or two calves which I'd a reared by this bull. So I just switched over to suckler cows. I went to Salisbury and bought some calves to put on the milking cows and that's how I started.

In my view all my cattle, whether it's cow or young stock, they ought to have a bit of Galloway in them. They're a hard breed. I remember I was down the field ditching one day and I could see these cows running across the Forest. I thought, what's on out there. I looked and watched them, they all got in a huddle. I thought there was one down; that's what I thought. So I went off to have a look. I couldn't believe my eyes: there were little seedling firs and they were eating them. I can't remember what time of year it was - it would be in the winter, or could have been in the spring - there was times of the year when those seedling firs have a sticky substance coming out. I think that's what it was they were after. It's the same with holly; they'll eat that.

Before the BSE problem[26], I kept most of the heifers. I'd let them run out, then when they were about 2 year old, bring them in, put them to the bull. Those that got in calf, OK, those that didn't they stayed there and got fat.

---

[26] Bovine spongiform encephalopathy (BSE), commonly known as mad-cow disease, is a fatal neurodegenerative disease in cattle that was first recognised in the UK in the late 1980's and caused a major crisis in British farming. It led to the slaughter of more than four million cattle during the programme to eradicate it as well as causing the deaths of several hundred humans who contracted a disease with similar neurological symptoms subsequently called vCJD, or (new) variant Creutzfeldt-Jakob disease.

They'd be up 3½ perhaps 4 year old before they went on for slaughter. Main of them ran in the Brockenhurst area. In the past I've picked them up in February and taken them straight on to Salisbury market. They had a bit of hay or straw, wheat at times, apart from that, nothing. I used to say they were organic and they used to laugh at me: but they *were* organic.

It was sort of on a ranching system. They were wild, and they just lived where others would starve. I remember, this particular heifer, she was a black Hereford: a Galloway with horns. We tried to catch her up in a corner down there at Wilverley. We got her in there and she went straight out over the other fence, across Wilverley Plain. We had to go back and get a horse to catch her.

The change from dairying would have been in the 'sixties, and the export of ponies was just beginning. I had a number of enquiries: one or two people came from abroad and asked about ponies. The thing was my father sent ponies all over the country and, I suppose the name stuck. When it comes to it, another reason I gave up dairying: Lennie didn't like it - he hated it. And I could see that life could be made easier. The thing was, I couldn't do both.

Export of New Forest ponies

Starting in the early sixties, Len took on the export of ponies with the knowledge and enthusiasm that he brought to all his business enterprises. He sold good quality youngstock and riding ponies to buyers across Europe, and ensured that they were well transported and arrived safe and healthy at their new homes. Together with two or three other New Forest breeders, he took many hundreds of ponies across the channel and was always content that he'd given them a chance to have a good life and spread awareness of the best qualities of the breed.

In the course of the sixties and seventies, he travelled widely across Sweden, France, Holland and Germany. He met and got on well with the local people, making a particular friendship with a Swedish buyer which lasted for many years. He became well known as a trustworthy and knowledgeable breeder of New Forest ponies and was a well respected judge at shows in several countries.

Pony export started in the late fifties: it only wants one to start it off. Holland was one of the first that did take the Forest ponies. But I found with the Dutch people, you never knew what they wanted. Then France came along, Germany. One of the first ponies I ever exported, must have been back in the late 50's and that went to the King of Nepal, through Mrs Parsons. They wanted a particular pony for the children to ride. It had to be black, jet-black. I happened to have one.

In those days we could sell ponies in France, or in Europe. These foals - I'm not saying little rough things - strong foals, could be sold out there for kids' ponies. There's people all over the world - there's people in this country - would love to buy their child a pony, but they haven't got the money. If I went to Beaulieu Road Sale and bought the - I won't say the very best foals - but foals which were good, sort of from £40 to £60, probably a bit more -- after all expenses were paid, I could sell them out there for round about £100.

With the Forest ponies over in France, Sweden and Germany, there's sort of a Mafia, they want to keep the price up - just a certain few want to keep the price up. There was a fellow I used to take a lot of ponies out to France. He tried to join the Stud Book. They wouldn't accept him because he was buying ponies at less money than they were. They were breeding ponies themselves, and they were a sort of a Mafia. It applies here too.

In France, they have a big fair there at a place called Lasse, it's opposite Tourissy. I've been there a number of times. I took a load of foals and sold them. There would have been a lot of people there: these foals, you could sell them like hot cakes. Just because they're going to France, a lot of people think they're going for meat. It's not the case. What happens to the ponies here?

I know, several years ago, it must have been before the minimum value came about, Ensors the auctioneers in Wimborne, used to do the valuations for me. This particular time, they were so busy they couldn't spare the time to come up. I told them, 'What I'll do, if I brought them down, you could do them on a market day - Wimborne Market day, after the market.' So that's what I did. Took them down, let them in the ring, and he valued them in the ring. Of course, it wasn't long before there were several people there.

Anyway, this person, someone must have said about them going to France. She came up and said, 'Are you taking these poor little things to France?' She let go at me. She had her husband with her. I said, 'Now look, Madam, I don't know you from Adam, but these ponies are going to France. If you want, you can come with me and I'll pay all your expenses. I've got nothing to hide. You can see where they go.' Anyhow, she calmed down. It's the same with the RSPCA: I asked Mr Stace to come with me a number of times, but he never did. It could have been the Society: he wouldn't be allowed to, I don't know.

These days, expenses are a lot more: the vet fees, then there's the ferry charge. But they could still be sold out there. Two years ago when the sales of Beaulieu Road ponies had dropped, I rang a friend of mine, who I used to take a lot of ponies out to. I rang him up and told him, I asked, 'Could I sell them out there?' He said yes, they could be sold there. If I was 20 or 30 years younger, I should do something about it again today. I know darned well they could be sold, but the minimum value beats you, that's what beats you. Like Sweden, I'm sure, well on the Continent altogether, I'm sure that they could be sold there but it's this minimum value.

I started to take ponies to France (I suppose that must have been the late fifties): this fellow came in one day: I could see it was a French car. He asked me who the ponies belonged to in the Forest. I told him - different owners. Then he said, 'Have you got some?' I said yes. 'Would you sell some?' I said yes. I took him round and I sold him a load. He told me what he wanted. He was a corn farmer, he'd done a lot of reseeding. He wanted the ponies to go over the reseeded areas to graze it off. A lot of the old farmers reckon it's better to graze it off than to cut it. He had several loads from me. I agreed a price: at first I didn't know what the ferry charge was. I had to find that out, which I did when he agreed to have the ponies. I took those ponies to France to Le Havre at £45 each. That was anything up to 3 year old - not foals, but 1, 2, 3 year olds. He called them store ponies. It's like we call store cattle you see. He grazed them on and they came up good ponies. Some were registered and some not: in those days they didn't bother much about registering them. Then the ferry charge, return for the lorry, was £53 - now it's about £500.

Then I sent 75 ponies - there were one or two Forest ponies and quite a lot of Shetlands - to Malta. That was a nightmare. I didn't go myself. The chap that bought the ponies, he arranged the transport, all I did was to supply him with the ponies, get them valued and they came and picked them up. It was quite a big lorry: took 25. They went over to France, through France to Aosta. There were 4 miniature Shetlands on this load; they were really small. They were quite valuable actually. Customs wouldn't let them go down through Italy. The vets at Aosta wouldn't let them go unless they had these 4 Shetlands. The driver rang me and told me, I said, 'No way. All the ponies got to go.' He said, 'Well they won't let us go.' I said, 'Well, what's the agent doing?' He said, 'He's supposed to be doing what he can.' I said, 'Let me think about it for a bit. You ring me in the morning.'

In the morning he rang up and I said, 'What I've done, I've arranged for you to go back into France and stay at a friend's place.' I mean these ponies were stood in that layerage; they wanted a rest. I told him where he had to go. So, he went back into France. I got in touch with the agent that I'd used for years and told him all about it. He asked me who the agent was, and I said I didn't know. 'All right,' he said, 'I'll do the job for you, I'll get them through.' They stayed on the farm there for about a fortnight, then they went and picked them up. They got to Aosta again. Do you know what, they wouldn't let those ponies go down through by lorry, they had to go by rail and the lorry had to go down through Italy empty!

They wanted money. This was what it was all about. That first load that went, I reckon, I don't know what it cost, but I reckon it was somewhere about £3,000. Anyhow, the next two loads went down through all right. They still had to go by rail. The Italians: they're devils!

Charlie Dovey was a great friend. We used to go up to Great Yarmouth together when the ponies were going to Holland. There was Charlie, Bob Andrews and myself, we'd all go up together, overnight. Charlie would take a load and Bob Andrews would take a load. I used to leave home about 9 o'clock at night and drive up to Staines and pull in there, let the traffic come out of London, then go right on up the North Circular Newmarket road. If we went up together, we weren't in the same vehicle, but I suppose it was company.

Beaulieu Road Sales in the 1960's

We had to be up there by 6 o'clock in the morning, because they had to go in layerage for several hours. I bet we hadn't been there long before you'd hear someone come down through: that was Miss Husky, she knew my father. She was one of these animal rights people, I think it was the International League for Horses, she was from. I know one time; it was after the Beaulieu Road Sale. She was always there all day. We went up that night with a load we already had ready to go. Next morning she was up there, too.

It was cruelty - that's what she was after. I used to get on alright with her, I mean you got to flannel them up a bit haven't you? I was up there one morning on my own and I heard someone coming. I guessed it was her. She tapped on the window. I said, 'Morning, Miss.' She replied, 'Oh, thought it might have been Mr Dovey.' I said, 'No, I don't think he's coming today.' I don't know why it was but she didn't get on too well with Charlie. I think he used to pull her leg so much. She said, 'How many have you got?' I told her and off she went. I suppose that was her job and that was it.

When we first started going up, we'd load them straight on the boat, load them straight down in the hold. But later on, they had to go in layerage for 10 hours. It was in a big barn - or 2 or 3. Funnily enough, it wasn't on the docks, it was about a couple of miles down the road. This chap that kept the layerage was a haulage contractor; he had cattle lorries. We had to wait and see till they were vetted, because sometimes there would be a reject. Then they had to come back. Luckily enough we never brought any back, but we had to be there in case, or one or the other of us. If there was three of us went up, two would go on home and the other one would stay there in case there were any rejects.

A Swedish friendship

Len's export of ponies gave him the opportunity to travel into Europe, meeting many people who became long term friends. One of his greatest friendships was with a man from Sweden who turned up on his doorstep one day and asked who the ponies belonged to. Len travelled to Sweden on many occasions and found the people kindly and hospitable. He taught his Swedish friends something of the Forester's knowledge of ponies – and he learnt a thing or two about pony keeping from them, too.

I'd been to Germany, Holland and France, but not to Sweden - with Sweden, you're that much farther away. I had sent some there previous to that, but to send ponies there was a bit of a hassle. A vet came and took blood and I had to send that blood up to Newmarket and they were all blood tested before they went. In those days, I had done it through the bloodstock agency. I used to send the blood up to them, they'd send it on to Newmarket, then they'd get the export license and whatever. Then they scrapped that for some reason; I don't know why.

Then one or two people from Sweden came over here and bought ponies. One day, out of the blue, midday, I was indoors having a sandwich and a cup of tea, and this car pulled up outside. I went out and this Swedish man said to me, 'Are you Mr Mansbridge?' I said yes. He said, 'We're over here on holiday, but I'm looking at the ponies as well. I was staying in a hotel in Chesterfield and was given your name.' I asked him who gave him my name. 'I don't know,' he said, 'but I found you. I'd like to buy some Forest ponies. Only there's a man in Sweden that says he's the only person that can buy New Forest ponies, but I'd like to buy some.' I said, 'If you wants some I can sell you some, all right. When do you want me to show you some?' 'Now,' he said.

So I went indoors and got a hat and coat, took him down to Don Stephens, when he was up at Twiggs Lane. He bought 3 off him. I took him then on over to Culverley to Charlie Dovey. He went out on Culverley Green and bought 3 more off him: 2 of those were skewbalds as a matter of fact. We got back out on the road and he stopped and he said, 'Mr Mansbridge I've come to buy some ponies off you, not other people. I haven't seen any of yours yet.' I said, 'All right we'll see them now.' I took him round on the Forest and he finished up with a load.

His name was Erik Gustavon. He said, 'I'll come in tomorrow morning and pay you for them and make final arrangements.' The next morning he came in with a darned great wad of notes: Swedish money, like the old white five-pound notes. I suppose I looked at them a bit old fashioned, he said, 'You don't know about this?' I said, 'Not really. I wouldn't know what that's worth.' He said, 'Where's your bank?' I told him and he said to go and talk to them. So I got the car and went down the bank. I saw the bank manager: he was all for it. He told me how many Krona to the pound that day, and that it was all right, they would take that money: that's what was worrying me!

I went back up home and Erik worked it all out, paid me what was due. He said to me, 'Now look, don't bank that money. Keep it for a few days and watch the rate of the Krona. Look in the paper every day and watch it. It's down now and it's going up gradually. Keep it maybe for a fortnight, perhaps three weeks and then put it in, and this money will earn money.' Which it did! I know on occasion, you could earn £100 or more, just on the money. He always did that, and nine times out of ten, I earned a lot of money on that money. It was good of him to tell me. He was straight as a gun barrel.

When he paid the first deal, he said to me, 'Well what have I got to give you something for taking me and buying these other ponies.' I said, 'Oh that's alright you've bought some off me.' 'Oh no, no, no I want to pay you.' He wouldn't accept no, so I thought and said, 'Well you give me £5 a pony if you're satisfied.' 'No, no, no,' he said, 'that's not enough. I'm going to give you £15 a pony, whether it's one or a hundred.' and he did.

He wanted ponies to live on the mountains - that sort of ponies. Then after that, he wanted them for breeding or riding. He sold them on again. He was a very wealthy man. He used to go timber hauling with horses in Sweden and Canada. He had a fair bit of property, and he sold some land to the government for a National Stud. He made a lot of money over that. They had many breeds of stallions there and they built a trotting racetrack. He had 2 or 3 racing trotting horses and he had one champion. He didn't often go racing but he had a trainer. The trainer would ring up and say, your horse is going to run today: he'd back it and he was pretty lucky that way.

I sent out two loads and then he wanted me to go out with a load, which I did. We went up the M1, I suppose it was, got some ways the other side of London and pulled in a lay-by. The chap who was driving said to me, 'Could you take over. I've been working all day: I'm tired.' I said all right. So, I took over. He told me the towns I had to go through. This particular day we went out from Hull. We were on the sea about 36 hours. After we'd been going a couple of hours I asked the driver of the vehicle about water. 'I think we ought to go and give them some water.' Water is more important than food. Carrying it down was the problem. You try carrying a bucket of water down the vertical ladders! I said, 'Have you got a rope on the lorry?' He had a rope, and we let it down like that.

We got there, went to Sweden, came back into Tilbury and, as we were coming into Tilbury dock gate with this chap driving, a policeman in front stopped him. He said, 'Oh not now! We've been to all the way to Sweden and back. Not now!' I said, 'Well, what's the matter?' He said, 'I haven't got any tax have I, and no operator's license.' And I was driving that lorry! Luckily, all it was - he stopped him because of some traffic on the road.

I got to know what Erik wanted; the type of animals he liked. Of course, he's like me, he likes them all. One day he rang me up, 'Bring out a load of ponies but I want one good riding pony, I want a very good riding pony.' I bought some ponies off Ralph Hayward and one of those seemed just right, a nice pony. They were all registered. I took them out there from Tilbury. After I'd parked the lorry, I went back to find the Captain. He knew who I was; he'd seen the papers no doubt. 'Mr Mansbridge with the horses?' I said, 'That's right. I've come to ask you a favour.' He said, 'What's that?' I said, 'Water for my horses.'

He looked at me. 'You're the first person that ever has asked me for water for their animals.' He shook my hand. He said, 'You'll have a hosepipe to your vehicle and there'll be a man, day or night, to give you a hand. I'll see the Purser. You just go and make final arrangements. While you're there, get a card off him for your duty frees.' So, that was that.

When you come off the ferry over in Sweden, there is a Customs man waiting for you. He takes you to the Customs warehouse and then he takes you up on a weighbridge to be weighed: the whole load. You then go on to the quarantine (this is in Gothenburg), to unload the ponies, clean the lorry out, put some new bedding in. Then you go back and weigh it, the lorry empty. There was a tax on the weight; they call it 'meat tax'. They do it all for you. When I dropped the ramp and let them out in the compound, Erik was one side of the ramp and I was the other. 'Mansbridge,' he said, 'What have you done with these ponies?' Well, it took the wind out of me; I thought how well they looked really. I said, 'I'm sorry, Sir, I don't know what you mean?' 'Well,' he said, 'You look as though you've come 20 mile down the road!' That's what I wanted to hear: it's the same, don't matter where. In France you're only on the boat 5 or 6 hours; when you're on there about 30 odd hours, it's a different story. Really speaking, you're not supposed to go down in the hold and look at them, but I did. During the night I'd go down 2 or 3 times.

All the registered New Forest ponies Erik had, after a few days, they were blood tested. The National Stud was only a couple of miles down the road from his little farm, on land he'd sold them. He used to take these ponies down there and get them blood tested to see if they were hot or cold blooded. If they were hot blooded they weren't Forest ponies. He gave me a list of different breeders, 'Never buy a pony off them for me,' he said 'They're hot blooded.' If he had one that was hot blooded, he wouldn't keep it very long.

We got on really well actually. I'd take ponies out there and I then took another load out. It would have been the fortnight previous I'd taken the other ones. He passed most of them on; well he passed practically all of them on. He also sent some ponies on to Finland from Sweden. You could sell riding ponies, not Forest run ponies but riding ponies, out there in those days. The type of pony what they really liked was sort of 14 up to 14.1 or 14.2, sort of Thoroughbred x New Forest that type of thing. They loved them. Of course, with the Forest ponies, we didn't want to take too many of them there, it would spoil the market that way. I don't know how many ponies I took out there for them. I would think in the region of 600 or 700, maybe more.

Exporting ponies to Sweden

Going back to this broken pony that Erik wanted special. It was dark when I got there, and he said, 'I'll go and get a saddle put it on and you can ride her round.' She was quiet; I got up on her and rode her round. I stayed there a few days (you couldn't always get back straight away: perhaps it was 4 or 5 days before you could get back). He said I'm going to take this pony to the person that wants him. Come on, you can come with me. Off I go.

When I got there I discovered the person the pony was for - discovered she was in Switzerland. I think it was a birthday present for her from her parents - she was a schoolteacher out in Switzerland. They liked the pony and they rang and got through to the daughter. They called Erik to the phone and he said to me, you could sell it to her. I didn't know if she'd speak English. Anyhow she did. I think she was a language teacher. I told her all about the pony, the colour everything. What ever she asked me. He gave me the price on a piece of paper, I said what the price was. Oh, that's OK, she was coming home in a few days. She was thrilled to bits with the pony. What I was going to say was, I took the pony to Sweden and when I got there I sold it to Switzerland!

Then I was taking a load of ponies out to his place one day, going up into the mountains: they're sort of gradual. As we were going up over these mountains, and I could see this pony in a field with a 9 or 10 year old girl. When I got up close I could see what pony it was. I pulled in the lay-by quite close and walked back to this pony and I said to the girl, I brought this pony to Sweden from England. She looked at me. I said, 'Her name is Warren Jessica, one of Charlie Dovey's breed.' 'Yes, it is!' she said. Of course, her mother must have seen me there with the horsebox talking to the kiddie: out she came. I said to her, 'I brought this pony to Sweden.' She could speak a little English - very little. I told her what I knew. I had to go and have a coffee then, didn't I!

I was there I should think nearly an hour, perhaps more. The kiddie could speak good English: the younger generation can, I think. I told her where I was going, staying overnight like. She said, 'When you come back call in and see us.' That's what happened, if I was back there at all, I'd just call in and say hello. Out there I found that I got on with the people quite well. I mean people I didn't know: if you were in difficulties, they'd help you. That's how they are in Sweden. I made many friends out there.

Funny thing -- something else happened. It was along the time there was a lot of Indian saddles coming in the country like. When he came over one day, I happened to have a couple there and he saw them. I told him they were very cheap only about £8 or £9 apiece like. He said, 'Oh, get some for me.' I did and I took them out there. A friend of his had a riding school, quite a big woman. He let her have some. Anyhow, he rang me again, told me he wanted some more ponies, he said, there's a surprise when you get out here. I didn't know what he meant or anything.

I went out there with the ponies and drove them overnight. Next morning I went straight out to this woman. Didn't she let me have it! A nail came up through one of these saddles (with those old Indian saddles you didn't know what to expect), came up into her backside! It was all in fun as you might say, but she just about let go, in Swedish! Of course I didn't understand her.

They had me there a few days afterwards, when they had a show there. There were all sorts of ponies there, including their local breed Gotland ponies. They're horrible things; I don't know how to describe them: they don't trot, they run. They're no more than 12 hands. I suppose the locals use them for working, but in this riding school they did use them to ride; but they're horrible things to ride.

I went and he said we're going to ask you to do something. I thought perhaps it might have been judging the Forest Ponies; that's what I thought. Anyhow, they had all these ponies going round in the ring, they took me out to see if I could pick out the Gotland ponies? I could to a certain extent - well I did. He was thrilled about it, that I could do it. Until I'd gone to Sweden I'd never seen a Gotland pony.

I've judged ponies all over Europe. I went out to Belgium judging the Forest Ponies, a few years ago. There were three of us judges: there was myself, a judge from Holland and a Belgian judge. The Dutch judge, before we started judging, was talking of different things. He told me that he also bred Dalmation dogs. I said, 'My father always told me, never to sell the best, always sell the second best. Well, if anyone comes to see ponies, I don't sell them the best.' 'Oh,' he said, 'Funny you should say that, I'm the same with my dogs.'

The ponies come singly into this compound and we judged them singly. The Steward announced the next pony coming in. It was one of Mr Hoyle's of Emery Down. He had a good line of ponies; he had some good ponies. I thought myself, 'This'll be a good pony.' When it came in the ring, you never saw such an object in all you life! Damned great head! Funnily enough, this pony was bought from Holland. That's how it came about. Anyhow, this pony came in, and as I say, it was an object! I tapped the Dutch judge on the shoulder and I said, 'What you told me earlier on about your dogs is right with the ponies. You sell your rubbish!' We got on quite well.

Gymkhanas, races and rodeos with New Forest ponies

Throughout his life Len's first love has been the breeding and riding of quality ponies, especially New Forest ponies. He rode in the Boxing Day Point-to-point from the time he was a boy until he was 75. His wife, Joyce, was also a keen breeder of New Forest ponies, and their children were brought up to ride from an early age. They were always keen to show, race or compete with their ponies and Len took a leading role in the organisation of a local gymkhana team. They went to shows and gymkhanas across the south of England and won a good number of rosettes and prizes.

With a small group of enthusiasts he organised race meetings all over the Forest, and started a rodeo for the brave and foolhardy to test their skill against the wiliness of unbroken Forest ponies. But his proudest memory was of meeting the Queen when she came to the New Forest as part of her Silver Jubilee celebrations.

Much of the money raised by the gymkhanas and races went to support the funds of the New Forest Commoners' Defence Association and the New Forest Pony Breeding & Cattle Society, on both of which he served as a committee member for many years. But Len enjoyed the competition and the spectacle too. He never tired of competing, and brought his children up to do the same.

When we were at Mullins the wife had a really good pony, Brandy, and Sheila had a skewbald pony, Jimmy. He was one of the last skewbald Forest ponies, because there were skewbalds registered at one time. He was a really good kid's pony, but Sheila wasn't really into it.

Marion had a pony called Strawberry: he was hell of a good pony. He was a Forest pony, but a little thick set pony. He was about 13 hands, an old type of Forest pony. Of course, he was strawberry roan. Out in the field you couldn't catch him: he'd go round. It was a laugh. You'd hear her down the field cursing. In the end, what we did, we left the headcollar on him with a long rope

Funnily enough, that particular pony, I tried to buy him one time, for her. The owner wouldn't sell him. He lived down Blackfield. Anyhow, it went on a twelve month, I suppose. About 11 o'clock one night he rang me up, 'You still want to buy that pony?' I said, 'Yeah.' He said, 'You'd better come and buy him.' I said, 'Alright, I'll come down tomorrow.' 'No,' he said, 'I want you to come now!'

Left to right: Marion, Lennie and Sheila on their ponies

I think what had happened, he had two children and they wouldn't do anything with the pony. I never found out the truth, but I think that's what it was. So I went and woke Marion up and told her. 'Alright,' she said, 'I'll come with you.' We went down there with the lorry and bought him. Gave him thirty quid for him, saddle and bridle.

I used to train the Pony Club - Prince Philip Team - for a couple of years. There was Lennie, Marion, Eric Dovey, Bobbie Dovey, Jimmy Haynes, Mary Jackson and another girl. Today, there's very few gymkhanas, but those days we used to go all over the place. One or two of the main shows we'd go to. We were the New Forest Group and did quite well really. They were a rough team, I can tell you. Cor', them nippers, didn't they used to give me a life!

Bobbie, he was about the quietest one in the team, you could put some sense to him. I used to train them on a stopwatch. Bending or whatever: do it on the stopwatch singly and try and get them to break their own time. I remember a time, I had a little pony, she was about 12.1 or 12.2. She was a miniature thoroughbred, just like a whippet dog. She'd nearly gallop away and leave them standing. Being small and with speed as well she was ideal for gymkhanas.

Marion would have been about 12; she was really keen, I will say that. More so than Sheila, the eldest daughter: she used to ride, she had her own pony, but she didn't like gymkhanas. Lennie didn't either; it was too slow for him (well, he had to do as he was told). We used to have some fun; I used to go off with them and join in, too. I remember one time down at Beaulieu, Mary Jackson, her mother ran a few gymkhanas. At one of them, I can't remember what it was in aid of now, they had pair jumping. Mary wanted to go in the pair jumping but didn't have a partner. She came up and asked me if I'd go in. I said, yes but I haven't got a pony. In the end I rode Marion's pony. Marion had already been in and she was in the final. I rode her pony in and we came in the final. The same pony was in the same final twice. When it came to it, Marion and her partner (I can't remember who her partner was), they had to beat us. They beat us and when I had to go and collect my prize I had to walk, didn't I!

Another time we went to a gymkhana down at Wimborne. Lennie went in one or two events but, as I say, he wasn't very keen. Lennie was entered for a Card Race. They had four chairs down the end of the ring, with four different cards – clubs, spades, whatever on each chair. You go down and pick up a card. Then you go back and sit in another chair. Anyhow, it ended up, I took Lennie's place on a pony he had called Peanut. He was a good pony - fast. Anyhow, I rode him and I finished up in the final. Marion was one of the other three in the final. I jumped off - leapt off the pony into the chair at the finish - and the chair collapsed with me, but Marion was second. As I was coming out there were two or three women saying, 'Fancy you beating your daughter. Why didn't you let her win?' I said, 'Look Madam, if I let her win, the next time she goes in with John somebody or another, she's going to think he's going to do the same. They've got to go all the way. That was my opinion anyhow.' It made her keener: she used to enjoy it.

The first time I rode in the Point-to-Point was 1929, perhaps 1930. It was a children's race. I've still got the cup I won, as far as I know: the date's on there. I've competed in the Point-to-Point - well, I was going to say every year - not every year - but practically every year after that until I was 74 or 75, I can't quite remember.

I've had 2 or 3 funny ones; I've had 2 or 3 accidents. One year I was leading on a pony we had in those days called Brown Jack. He was a good pony. I rode him in the Point-to Point, 2 or 3 times, and this particular day I was way out in front. Like a damned fool I looked round to see where the others were and I went in a clay hole: tipped upside down. That was down along by Milkham, on the Broomy road. I'll never forget that day. It was cold. I had blood streaming down my face. I was second and after I weighed in, I went over to a pool of water on the Forest, got my handkerchief out and bathed it. Then I went back and the doctor put 9 stitches in my face.

Then I came down another time: that was not much better than a clay hole. It was a way across the Forest coming out of Burley in towards Wilverley, right on the edge of the Golf Course, at Greenbury Bridge. It goes down very steeply and this particular pony jumped from the top to the bottom. As I went over the bridge, he changed his leg, put his foot in a hole and tipped upside down. He rolled over on top of me and cracked four ribs; that was rather uncomfortable. Funnily enough, it was Lennie's pony, bred by old Bob Kitcher; but I never liked the pony. I never liked him! There it is, experience is the best teacher.

The Point-to-Point is run by the Breeding Society. Over the years I've done the races and rodeos and put a lot of money into the Breeding Society. The rodeo was started at Romsey. One or two locals - the undertaker there was one of the organisers. That's where it started and we carried on. We did quite well: it was all fun. I supplied some ponies for it. I won't say they were all Forest ponies, but mainly.

People stayed on, occasionally - not for long. They had a way of bucking, if they kept going straight it wasn't so bad but they'd buck three or four bucks and then all at once drop a shoulder and out you'd go. That's happened to me with horses many a time.

I remember one rodeo, I didn't have enough ponies I really wanted to use, but I had a load of ponies that was going to Sweden couple of days after. I had the export license, they were tagged and everything to go, finished up I used those. I just took a chance that none of them broke a leg. I mean, if one or two of them had broke a leg, I'd have been up a tree!

Rodeo at New Park, Brockenhurst in the 1980's

130

We had a few donkey races for the kids as well. One year I didn't have enough, so I rang a friend of mine up at Chichester that I knew had donkeys; he used to take them on the sands. I asked him if there was any chance of borrowing some for a couple of days like. He agreed, he said, you've got to give me a tenner for my trouble, which I did. After that I used to go down Chichester and pick up half a dozen donkeys and give him the tenner. Come back and I'd take them back the next day. That was all out of my own pocket like.

Also, we used to have a barbeque there. Frank Terry used to do that, roast a pig: that was his job. It all made money for the Society, but you get very few offer to lend you a hand. When we had a Committee Meeting, I've asked if anyone had a pony I could pickup and use for that. I never had one offer. It was just myself that supplied the ponies and the Alford brothers over at Winsor. I was annoyed about that because all the money we made was split: half went to the Commoners' Defence and half went to the Breeding Society. I don't know: the Society don't appreciate those things you know. You never get any appreciation: but there it is. It was good fun, I'm not disputing that at all.

I remember one event, we made about £1,000. Finished up, just over £400 each. I gave the £400 to the Breeding Society and I said I wanted that money put to one side, either invested or put to one side for a rainy day. I'd heard through the grapevine something was happening. I thought, well you won't use that money to help the studs: I didn't think that was a good use for it. I never said anything to any of the committee about what I'd done. I think they were rather flabbergasted, but in the end I was asked by Mrs Wright if that money could be used for Beaulieu Road. I agreed, that is what I wanted it for, things like that. For it to be kept for a rainy day, repairs to Beaulieu Road Sale or something like that.

After I stopped riding in the point-to-point, I started doing the collection. I started it one year and then my grandaughter carried on; it was her pony we used. I had a box made: it went from there. I think it's around about 20 years I've collected. Nearly always it's up round about £200. It wasn't always over, but not too far away. You know the Breeding Society is now a charity, therefore, you've got to, or the Society has got to comply with charity commission rules, which really speaking, we weren't! I brought this up at a meeting and they just treated it as a joke, but I'd made enquiries, one or two different things that had to be done, but most of the committee treated it as a joke. I didn't like it at all. It was me, I was doing the collecting. I could have run off with that money just like that. You know, if you're on a committee and you don't do things just as you should do, I'd rather not do it.

You could get into trouble without asking for it. What started this off, about 2 years ago, 3 years ago perhaps, I was collecting and there were these two fellows - well dressed, very well dressed. They put a few coppers in, then they started asking me questions. I thought to myself, what do they want to know that for? Then I thought about it, I still believe they had something to do with the charity commission, it could have been. That is when I brought it up at committee, but it was like water off a duck's back. That is one of the reasons I packed it up. There was that and the tradition broken, and I didn't like it at all. As regards the tradition of setting the route for the Point-to Point, that was a gentleman's agreement made by the founders of the Point-to Point, so in my opinion, the council of today, has got very little respect for the council of that day, if you follow me. Maybe I am old fashioned: I'm glad I am.

I suppose one of the proudest moments, or proudest days, of my life was when I met the Queen. That was on Whitefield Moor when she came to the Forest for the Silver Jubilee. We had a pony parade on Whitefield Moor arranged by the Breeding Society. The agisters were in front, leading, and they drove through into Whitefield Moor. She got out and walked round the parade of ponies, then they got up and went off again. I had a stallion and she came up to me and spoke to me, well to be quite honest, I just didn't know what to say. Funnily enough, she asked me the name of the pony, I told her. Actually, this stallion I had then was one I bought, Peaover Sampson his name was. She looked at me and laughed and said, 'Very apt!'

She moved on, but one of her aides stopped and we had quite a chat, the remainder of them they were more than 100 yards away when he went. He asked me about the Forest ponies and one or two different questions. I told him to the best of my knowledge. He did say when he went, 'I'd like to say more but....' He couldn't stay any longer; they were just moving all the time.

New Forest ponies: changing times

Len's love of the New Forest dates back to his earliest days when he learnt from his father what to look out for in the land and its animals. He took great pride in the breeding of both his ponies and cattle and retains fond memories of the older type of New Forest pony, noted for its hardiness and good temperament. With age comes the sadness that the life we enjoyed as children and strong young commoners is gone and there is nothing we can do to bring it back. Times change and so do the markets for commoned livestock and products. The small but sturdy, 'old fashioned' New Forest pony is no longer saleable, any more than the hardy cross bred house cow, or the wild Galloway cows that Len bred. The market is for bigger, finer ponies that will do well in the show ring, but will never survive a winter on the New Forest.

Over the years Len has seen the New Forest breed change and, in his opinion, not for the better. Nowadays he sees the breed as too refined; it has lost its hardiness, and the stallions have lost their masculinity. The modern market and the management techniques employed to make the Forest acceptable as a place of nature conservation and leisure mean that the traditional Forest and its traditional ponies, as well as the commoners who lived with them, are in danger of becoming a thing of the past.

Today the main of the ponies have lost their hardiness. The stallions have changed so much over the years. They are getting lighter boned; too much daylight under them. Years ago, at a stallion show or a stallion passing, the old judges or inspectors, they'd just look at them: they'd see if they had enough bone or not. If they weren't sure, then what they did, they'd run their hand down; but now they measure them. Another thing, I know they take blood from them, when they're inspected or after they're inspected, but, as I see it, they only take the blood to compare it with to see if that pony is by that horse, not to see if it's hot or cold blooded. Today, in my opinion, I don't think they're good ponies - well, they are, but they've got too elegant.

I don't suppose there's hardly any left of the old type, but probably the best old type forest pony would be bred by Mrs Vye. Then Mrs Corbett, she had a good old type of forest pony. They didn't live out, she bought 2 or 3 off Ted Burry. They didn't live on the forest – they did at one time.

There's no doubt, the Kitcher family - George Kitcher down Fuzzie[27] and old Jess Kitcher - they had a good line of ponies: they kept what they wanted to keep. Old Bill White, at Lyndhurst, I think he probably had one of the best lines in the Forest. And his line of breeding was a good line. Marchant from the Waterloo Arms Lyndhurst used to have a lot of ponies. Then they sold out and that's how it was. They were the old fashioned type of pony. All home bred, his own line.

Then Father he used to buy a lot of ponies from Charlie Dibben, he used to buy a lot of ponies off of him. Those ponies, he had some good ponies, the real old fashioned type of forest pony. He used to have several red roans, they were really nice ponies. The red roans are sort of dying out. They're an old breed , an old line. They had not a flaxen mane but more of a silver flaxen mane and tail. They were hardy ponies.

There are one or two red roans about. Miss Mangin, she had one, he was running outside of our place, up through Longwater. He died, 12 month ago, less than that I suppose. There are one or two of them left about, but very few. It's a line of breeding that should have been kept.

It's like myself with my cattle: well it took me years to get the breed about right to live on the Forest all the year round. I've got there! Now and again I get one that doesn't, but that line I'll get rid of. This is going to be the problem with this scheme[28], the lines they're going to get lost. I think it has got to be done very carefully. There's very few people that would have any bloodlines of Denny Danny and Spark. Spark was one of Bertie Peckham's; he had some good ponies – Newtown Spark. Then there was Broomy Slipon: I had two or three stallions by him. One, Ashurst Slipon was by Broomy Slipon, another one was Ashurst Apollo. We've got one or two lines of those and also Denny Danny, because they were outside of home at one time. Before the War, there were no studs, the only stud that I remember was down at Bucklers Hard, Mrs Hewlett-Campbell. They ran a riding school and they did breed Forest ponies; they had some on

---

[27] Furze or gorse, pronounced 'Fuzz' locally

[28] Here he refers to the Stallion Scheme, introduced in 2002 to reduce the number of foals born on the Forest. The number of stallions turned out each year to the present has been strictly limited. There is concern that the number and variety of bloodlines in the Forest run ponies will be reduced as a result.

the Forest. That's the only ones that I can remember that kept them in. As regards the studs today, practically all of them came to the Forest to get their foundation mares. They're forgetting this.

Years ago, I used to put Forest ponies on a farm at Nursling, grazing out the water meadows. I never paid anything. The farmer asked me if I'd put them there and I did, for several years. It started off with this chap's father actually; Fred Pearce, then he died and it was Tom Pearce. I used to take them over there; he'd ring up end of October and say, bring some ponies over. They'd eat out all the rough grass, eat it right down. He'd graze them on the water meadows along the Test and he always said that those ponies would do a lot more good than a man could do.

I had another friend, between Wimborne and Dorchester. Over the years I used to sell him heifers and calves. He said to me one day, 'I've got a field about 2 miles away from the farm, I don't know what to do with it. It's all stinging nettles and docks.' I said, 'Well, I wouldn't mind having that.' He said, 'What would you do with it? I told him I'd put some ponies in there. He jumped in his car and he took me. It was a field of about 8 or 9 acres. I looked at it. There was some grass there, but it was all old; it hadn't been used for several years. He'd bought this field and had never put anything in it because there were lots of stinging nettles. I said to him, 'If you let me have that field rent free until the end of March, I guarantee there won't be nothing here: it'll be eaten right out.' He let me have it in the end. I took a couple of loads of ponies down there and they had everything - there was nothing left. When we got them out I said, 'I'll bring these ponies back here next year. They want to be here for 2 or 3 years.' He let me put them there again for 3 years in the winter. That made that field and the ponies did all right on it, too.

It's the same with the village greens. Throughout all the villages around the Forest, they were all mown like a lawn. The Forest ponies did that. Since so many have been fenced out of the Forest, the council's spending millions to do that when the Forest ponies did it for nothing.

They keep on saying today, there's too many ponies on the Forest. I remember the time when there was as many again. At Lyndhurst, I remember on the Bench they used to stand up and shade[29] outside what was the Grand Hotel, opposite the fire station. Stand up under those trees and shade. Farther on up the end of the street at the Fox & Hounds there'd be a few more there. Then outside The Crown, there'd be some more there. Up through the High Street there could be 20 or 30 perhaps more, and round where the Police Station is today there'd be another 20 or 30 stood up in the road there, shading.

New Forest Commoners' Defence Association and Verderers' Court

Besides running his holding and his haulage business, Len was always deeply involved in the politics of the New Forest. He had been born in the Forest, he knew many miles of it intimately and he loved it. As a boy his father introduced him to the power and complexity of the relationship between the commoners and the Crown in the form of the Verderers Court. He was fascinated by it, and the ways in which the lives of the commoners could be influenced for good or ill by the actions of powerful bodies with whom they had to negotiate.

He was a committee member of the Commoners' Defence Association for 50 years, and always stood up for the rights of the Forest and its commoners, even if that meant standing on his own. In 1989 Len was asked by Joan Wright and Tim Moore[30] if he would stand as an elected Verderer. Although he was already over 70, he took on the challenge of standing for election. Even without canvassing, he won a seat, and found a new way of fighting for the cause of commoning and the survival of the New Forest.

The first Verderers' court I went to, it was in my school days. I think I was about 12. One Monday morning – the court was held Mondays then – seven o'clock, I got my bike out ready to go to school. Father came along; he'd been in the yard. 'Oh', he said, 'No need for you to go to school today. You can come with me. You'll learn more with me than

---

[29] 'to shade' is a local term to describe the way that New Forest ponies gather in certain places to catch a breeze in hot weather, so that the nuisance of flies is reduced.
[30] Joan Wright was chairman of the New Forest Pony Breeding and Cattle Society and Tim Moore was the chairman of the Commoners' Defence Association.

you will at school.' Never said where he was going or anything. I had no idea. About half an hour afterwards off we went in the car. At the time he had an old T-Type Ford pickup. We went to Lyndhurst and he parked his old car in the Crown yard and we walked back across the road into the Court. There's a picture in my head that will never be seen again. Opposite the court – there's a sort of a layby there – there were 3 or 4 horses and trucks – Forest trucks. They were commoners that worked in the Forest. They'd probably been pulling out some timber or something. There were quite a lot of bicycles, 2 or 3 ponies and carts, and some ponies with saddles and bridles on. I still didn't know what it was – he never said it was a court or anything. My father was like that. Inside the court, that hall was packed with commoners. I've never seen so many people since in the court.

I mean, at the time, I didn't know what was going on. In the end, as the Court progressed I learnt. It was the November Court and they were there asking for an extension for the pigs - an extension of the pannage season - and the commoners, they supported one another. When the Offical Verderer opened the Court, he said, 'I want all the presentments not connected with the pannage season.' I suppose he realised it was going to take time, because he could see all these commoners, and that's what happened. It went on. It finished, I think, somewhere about 4 o'clock.

They got to lunch time – I don't know whether it was half past twelve or one o'clock and they stopped for lunch. Some of the commoners went over to the Crown, had a pint of beer and their bread and cheese. Some went down the Fox and Hounds, and some just sat on their trucks. The Verderers went over to the Crown for lunch. And I had a glass of lemonade and packet of chips! So, it was an experience.

Two o'clock, Court started again and that's when the pannage season was brought up – they were asking for an extension. There were quite a lot of acorns about (my opinion always has been – that the pannage season should start a bit earlier, so the pigs can pick up the acorns – that is green ones. I have mentioned it a time or two, but never got anywhere). One had asked for an extension for a fortnight, another one three weeks, another one a month and, as I say, they supported one another. Well, that doesn't happen today.

I will say I listened to what was going on, and the thing was the commoners supported one another. Anyhow, it went off and the court was closed. I think it was about half past four. So after that – I mean I was still at school - but after that, if I had the opportunity, I'd go up and sit down and listen.

My father said I would learn more with him. It's the experience. Many times, when I've told him about something that happened, he'd say, 'That's experience.' I'm not so sure about the Verderers' court today. I do realise that Oliver Crosthwaite Eyre is doing the best he can but he wants some support, and today the court is over in about, less than an hour. There's something wrong somewhere. I do feel maybe, some of the Forest schools, possibly town schools, could take a number of children to the Verderers' Court. I think - my opinion - that would be some really good education. I mean, as I say, a lot of people don't know it's there.

And, well then I got more involved in the Forest - the Commoners' Defence and that. I was on the committee of the Commoners' Defence for just over 50 years, so it must have been about '46 or '47 when I joined. We came here '47, so must – no must have been '48. There was a person that lived at Marchwood at the time was a member. I was talking to him one day and he said, 'Why don't you join?' And I said I hadn't thought about it. And anyhow, when the election came up, he put my name forward. That's how it happened. I don't think I ever regretted joining it.

Then one time, I can't remember what the presentment it was I had to make – I was asked to do this by the Commoners' Defence - and I don't mind telling you, my knees were knocking, but I got on very well and it broke the ice. In those days the Verderers were mainly gentry. I can't really remember who, but I believe Sir George Mountford, Mark Powell and O. T. Price, and - I think - Mr. Gossling, who was the farmer at New Park. And, as I say, I can't remember the others. For a few times I was really a bit nervous. There isn't anything to be afraid of: but then, when you're not very old, there is!

If I remember rightly, the chairman of the CDA when I joined the committee was Major Ziegler. Then, he finished Tim Moore took on and we got on well together. I remember, on one or two occasions we had meetings up at Lyndhurst at the Grand Hotel. At one (I can't remember what that was about now[31]) there were 2 or 3 members of parliament there. Tim Moore said, 'Come on. I want you to be with me.' We chatted to them, and I think we put them in the picture. As I say, it was very interesting. I met a number of MPs that way and, we worked together. I don't think we had any cross word at all. We got on very well. If we had a problem, we sorted it out. And it was an experience.

I must say with Tim Moore, he was a leader. There's no doubt whatsoever. If Tim Moore got his teeth into something he wouldn't let go! I used to go down to his house at Alderholt and have a meeting there between ourselves. I was vice chairman for a number of years …. I can't remember how many.

Over the years a lot of things came up that we had to deal with. I was on the committee when the 1964 Act was passed and the perambulation was to be fenced. It was always said that the New Forest perambulation was from the River Blackwater right around the coast down to Christchurch. But now, you look at it today. I remember the perambulation of the Forest from Totton to Lyndhurst Road – where the Forest starts now, has been moved 4 times during my life time. For example, down the Woodlands Road, all that area each side, I understand now that's not in the perambulation of the Forest. Apparently, they tell me now the perambulation is the inclosure fence which is absolutely wrong. I always thought to move the perambulation had to be an act of parliament. That area, each side, before the roads were fenced was grazed down and you'd be surprised the arguments I've had over that with one or two. Down on my opinion, when the roads were fenced the acres of grazing land we lost through and Ashurst, and up the Woodlands Road would be somewhere about 150 to 200 acres.

I knew Hugh Pasmore before he was ever a Verderer. My father ran a riding school at Longdown, and he was one that used to come out most Wednesday's for a ride. Three of them, if I remember, used to come out. He was a clerk to Sawbridge's, the estate agents in Southampton. They opened an office at Lyndhurst and that's where Hugh Pasmore worked. When Mr Sawbridge died, Hugh Pasmore had it in his lap.

---

[31] Tim Moore thinks that the meeting was about drainage in the Forest

Hugh Pasmore was the one that brought the perambulation back out of Totton. Days gone by it was just this side of the coast: that marsh at Totton. As you go over the bypass, where the tar works are, there's marsh on the right: it runs right back. It's about 50 odd acres. I was given permission to put ponies down there. I did a little bit of investigating. Up at Queen's House the Verderers have got an atlas: I got permission to look at it. That marsh down there had 49 rights. It was a tithe marsh and, of course, the different holdings around the area, had rights on that marsh. That's what they paid their tithes fee for. It's either 47 or 49 plots which have got rights down there. It belonged to the Barker Mills estate, but two or three plots were sold off. People died and it's forgotten. And it just shows: on that atlas, I came across one or two places in Millbrook that have got Forest rights.

Down at Hanger Corner we fenced, or put a gate on, all the openings to the Forest to keep the ponies back out of Totton. Before that I wouldn't know how many times I went to Totton pound and got ponies out. We came all the way through up to Fletchwood and put a gate across and the fencing round the hospital and the cricket pitch. There's a driftway that runs from Ashurst cricket pitch right down through to Deerleap and the animals used to work all round the manorial waste and up Chapel Lane.

There's several acres of manorial waste there and there's a right of way from Ashurst cricket pitch down through by the keeper's cottage, right to Deerleap. We always called it the 'Driftway'. The animals could go from Ashurst, right round to Deerleap. We lost the cricket pitch. We lost all that grazing down through that we used to call the Back Way. If you go to the car park at Deerleap and up to the sand pit you'll see a post both sides of the road, and there's a bank goes right back through to the end of the manorial waste. This side is Forest, that side is manorial waste. I once suggested to put a fence up along the top of this bank, right through so the animals go right round, but they wouldn't listen.

David Stagg was a wonderful man. He was the commoners' friend. A lot of them didn't realise it, but he got that ground back down near the hospital at Ashurst. Anthony Pasmore always said, it's not Forest, it's Crown lands. Anthony Pasmore and myself have had no end of arguments about that from Ashurst cricket ground. I was born there. He was born in Southampton!

Then there's a lane at the end of Staplewood Lane, where it finishes at the Beaulieu Road in Longdown. In my opinion it would be 4 or 5, perhaps 6, acres. That grazing's gone - where, years ago, the animals, winter time especially, went down that lane to shelter. Not only that, from Staplewood Lane there was 6 or 7 commoners put their cattle through this lane and then there's 3 or 4 down the Longdown Road. They all went up through this lane to the Forest. I remember when 150 animals went up through there practically every day. They came from the holdings down Staplewood Lane. Then there was one in Marchwood, and there was another one, the postman at Pooks Green, Mark Dunning – his house cow. She never went far, just hung up through Staplewood Lane. But she had the right to go right the way up through Staplewood Lane.

The lane locally is called Balls Lane (I've got a map here somewhere; it shows that lane goes right up to the Forest). It was their right of way and, that's gone. You see, this is what does annoy me and it shouldn't be. That lane is Forest. I brought this up at the Commoners' Defence one night. It was one of the last things I tried to do, and how I didn't explode I don't know, but the person that was to benefit most, objected to it: a commoner – or he calls himself a commoner - but this is what's happening in the Forest. People coming in. If on these sort of occasions it is not objected to, in a minute, it'll go. I wouldn't be at all surprised one day, a multi-millionaire will come along, and he'll buy the Forest. And the Forestry Commission will sell it.

Down here at Ashurst I knew the Forest boundary. There was a big house down right by the railway: it was a guest house and the owner died. It was put up for sale and Hugh Pasmore had the dealings of it. Out in front of it – next to where they put that bridge – there was about half an acre of land that belonged to the Forestry Commission. It was right in front of this house – and it went on for years. It always stuck in my ribs about it. I got to hear that someone had bought it. There's 2 houses on it now.

When they put the Fawley bypass in, we fought hard to stop it. I suppose something had to be done, but the animals have a right on to go on the Forest throughout the Forest. That means that the animals have got a right on the A31 and A35. I know there's arguments the other way, but I've claimed for animals which have been killed on the fenced roads.

I remember one accident involved some pigs. It was the pannage season – 2 sows and pigs, it was – quite big pigs. I let them out from here and they used to come back at night. But they must have got on a wander – this is what happens: pigs wander off. And I think they got down by the fence on the main road and they found a way up to Lyndhurst, went through the underpass and then, of course, time of day was getting on and they couldn't find a way back. They went into what was the Nature Conservancy office (the old police station). At the back of that there's a piece of land which is enclosed (what for I don't know, but I've complained about it many times, but they went into this area). The gate was open and they found a way out through onto the road (not all of them, but some of them). I think it was four pigs were killed and one was injured, if I remember rightly. The person that hit them lived down at Players Crescent and he worked up at Lyndhurst. He was going home.

He was only a young chap, and he came to me claiming for the damage to his car, which was about a hundred, two hundred odd pound. He gave me the bill. I nearly paid it and then I thought I ought to have a word with Dennis Weston, the claims secretary. 'Well,' he said, 'We're going to have a bit of fun here. We'll claim for the pigs.' And I said to him, 'Well, can we?' He said, 'Well, the Forest animals have got a right on all the roads inside the perambulation, so, we'll claim.' He claimed and they lost the day, so they had to pay me for the pigs. This must have been back in the seventies. I can't remember exactly, though I know at the time there was a bit of dispute over it.

Old Charlie Dovey he told me (it wasn't long before he died). He said to me, 'Don't you ever forget the animals got a right on all the roads inside the perambulation.' So, I believe he's right, because these insurance companies wouldn't pay out if it wasn't right. I mean, none of us likes to paying for anything, do we?

Then we had a few battles with the Forestry Commission. What I say as regards the Forestry Commission is, during the war there was very little maintenance done and that's carried on ever since. For instance, I had a cow killed down on the railway a month ago now. Apparently – I haven't been to look at it – they took photographs of where she went through – there's just one strand of wire down the bottom there and she, a big cow – a Simmental cow – was hit by a train. And I did have a sow hit on the railway once before, because there have been noises about that railway fence for years. It must have been 15, 16 years ago, there was a complaint through the Commoners' Defence about the fence – which was poor. The complaint was made to the Forestry Commission and we decided to have a meeting. Will Parkes was to inspect it and I was given the job to go with him, from Lyndhurst Road Station to Whitley Ridge, one side and then the other side. The first day we started off at Lyndhurst Road and we walked down to Tuckers Bridge, the other side of Woodfidley, and we came back. On both sides out through Bishops Ditch area you have to get up on the railway to get through and I remember, when we went back I kept walking on: I had wellingtons on. In my opinion, Will Parkes never knew there were such places in the Forest! The next day we went on down from Tuckers Bridge to Ogborne and down through the inclosure. We had bracken right up five, six foot high -- had to push it out the way to see the fencing. Anyhow, it was done and I reported back. But they have never did a lot to that fence.

Then, out the back here – at Inner Sandhole, on the other side of the line, there's a drain which used to take all the rain water from the houses which were at Sandhole. They used to call it the Cutting. It goes right through the Forest actually. At any rate it goes along, I don't know, 2, 3 hundred yards, alongside the railway. Then it goes under the railway into a ditch out on the Forest which then runs into Beaulieu River. The lengthsmen on the railway kept the ditch cleaned out and kept the water running. I don't know whether it was part of their job or whether they did it on their own. There was one, two three - three lengthsmen. There were 3 cottages at Sandhole and three of the lengthsmen lived there and I think probably they did it for their own benefit, because, as I say, this water was rain water from the houses. When they packed up it just went.

In this ditch there was a lot of – well we call it – running sand, sort of quicksand. Now it's just a bog. But there was this little – it wouldn't be so wide as this room - a little causeway over this ditch. But there's no maintenance been done for years, and its gradually trodden and washed away. Consequence is, there's left a big hole and I've lost 3 cows in there. They go down in and there's clay at the bottom, so they can't get out. It's well over 3 foot deep where its washed away and they just get stuck in the clay. It's rather hidden from the railway and of course, no-one noticed them. Last one was a Charolais, a big Charolais, second calf cow and I was annoyed about that. I brought it up at the Court - made a presentment about it. Nothing's ever been done. Well, I say nothing's been done. I happen to know one of the men that was sent there to do something. They went there, and a shop steward came along and said, 'Oh, this don't need doing.' And it wasn't. All they did was cut a few bushes back. And, it's never been touched since.

So it's still there, and animals will still get stuck. They tried to tell me the ditch never was there. I said, 'I went over that before you were thought about !' I mean, I lived at Longdown. I was born there, and I knew that area like the back of my hand. If it was only a tree missing, I knew it. That is the trouble. Well, I don't need to tell you, in the Forest today there's people come here, telling us what to do. The trouble is, when they get a foot in: they come here 5 minutes and we've probably been here several generations.

I had no intention of being a Verderer. How that came about, it was coming up to the election and there was a meeting between the Commoners' Defence and the Pony Society. After the meeting Tim Moore and Joan Wright and me went over and had a cup of tea in the café nearby. We got talking about the election and Joan Wright looked at me, said, 'Why don't you put up?' I think it was about 10 days or a fortnight before the nominations closed. I said, 'You must be joking!', and well, I'd never given it a thought. I was interested in the Commoners' Defence: I was learning all the way there – about the Forest, and if something came up I heard it. But, in the end, they talked me into it.

The next day I went up and saw Mrs Blick. She was surprised – much as I was I think. I must say, she gave me all the help she could and did all the paperwork for me. The paper – the application – had to go to Winchester – Kennedy's the solicitors, by 12 o'clock this certain day. I went in the office and handed it in! Anyhow, then the election came along – I did no canvassing – Mrs Blick said to me about it. I said, 'Look if they don't know me now they never will.' I never asked them to vote for me - they used their own discretion. There was Vic Dukes, Jeff Kitcher and myself and – election day – when the results came out Jeff Kitcher had 2 more votes than me. I think it was in 1989. I've got a photograph somewhere of the first day I was on the Court and one or two members of the family supported me. My sister's son, from Australia and his wife were over on holiday; they came, and Uncle and his wife came and, of course, Marion and Brian[32] were there. I've got a photograph of that somewhere, I don't quite where.

Len and family outside the Verderers' Court (L-R Marion and Brian Ingram, Ivy and Dan Mansbridge, Leonard)

---

[32] Marion's husband, retired Senior Agister, Brian Ingram

It was when Lord Manners was the Official Verderer. We got on very well, and David Stagg, he always sat next to me on my right and he was very, very knowledgeable – in my opinion – and we got on well. But I can tell you being a Verderer, there are times when you're on your own. I don't know what it is, but the other Verderers seems reluctant to give you support, if you understand what I'm saying.

Charlie Dovey was a Verderer before me and he said to me one day, after I'd been elected, he said, you'll be on your own, you know. Anyhow, I said what I thought, and what I thought was right – whether it was right or whether it was wrong, I mean, but – I always sort of stood by my convictions. And, as I say, Lord Manners, I got on very well with him. I went out with him on different meetings and we got on very well.

While I was a Verderer the Lyndhurst bypass came up. That was quite a game. There was a second route planned down the side of the race course, which I think was the one that we'd agreed to, but they wanted to go over the Bench. In my opinion that was absolutely out of order, because if that route had gone behind the cemetery, over the years the Bench would get built on. Bolton's Bench is known throughout the world. And, well you probably know there's a bit of history about that. All I can tell you is what I've been told. I was told that a Captain Bolton was a regular huntsman, and his favourite horse died and he got permission to bury it on that green. On the right hand side along the Beaulieu Road, there's a hole (this is what I'm told) and that was all taken up there and made Boltons Bench. And when they'd got the big mound they planted the yew trees there and the bench goes right under the yew trees.

One old commoner that used to tell me about it was John Golden. He was an old commoner that had ponies – he only had ponies - and his prefix was Bench. He lived in a house near the Stag Hotel (next to the Stag there's the Mailman's, and there's a house next to that). He was well known throughout the Forest. I've never seen him on a horse, but when they drove in ponies, he was always there. If I remember rightly, he worked for Mr. Ernie Harris who was landlord at the Stag. Ernie Harris had a farm at Lyndhurst: Pinkney Lane – Angels Farm. He also had another farm down at Cadland and he took Dilton Farm. I can remember at one time John

Emms[33] stayed at the Stag quite a lot and, I understand through hearsay, if he couldn't pay for his board and lodging he gave Ernie Harris a painting. And, it's about half right, I think. When George Harris, the son, went to Australia, they took all those paintings, of course, and he had quite a lot of them. And, well, today they'd be very, very valuable.

Myself, I wouldn't give an inch of the Forest away. As a matter of fact, throughout my life, then if I'd had anything to say, I've said it. When I was Verderer, down at Sway, at Mead End (I think they call it Boundway Hill) there's a driftway. Over the years, the animals from Sway came up Boundway Hill, then down through this driftway out on the Forest. Well, down the back of this, there was a cottage with a couple of acres. It's called Driftway Cottage. Lord Manners brought it out at the meeting after the open court: the Forestry Commission had sold this driftway to the owners that had bought the Driftway Cottage. I jumped up and opposed it. I got no support from other elected Verderers and that told me I was on my own. Anyhow, it carried on: a meeting was arranged by the Forestry Commission. The land agent, John Booth the agister, myself, and - there was a bit of a job to get another – but Major Bailey he stood in and attended the meeting. If I remember, he was the Forestry Verderer. Anyhow, the Forestry had sold this driftway which was a right of way for the commoners in that area - for their animals to drift down through to the Forest.

Before the meeting I went down in that area and spoke to quite a number of old commoners (I sort of done my homework). Well, the owner of Driftway Cottage had already put in planning permission for 2 garages on Forest ground and over in the corner was a little brick building. It was a woodshed. And I made enquiries about that. This building was erected by the person that lived in the cottage before, and he erected it on Forest ground. I think his name was Rickman.

Unfortunately, I was about 5 minutes late for the meeting. I got behind a couple of tractors and trailers and when I arrived Major Bailey said,

---

[33] John Emms (1844 to 1912) was famous for his paintings of horses and dogs and, following his marriage to Fanny Primmer of Lyndhurst in 1880, lived for the rest of his life in the New Forest

'We've settled it.' 'Oh yeah.' I said, 'What have you done, then?' 'Well,' he said, 'We no longer think that it is of any use to the commoners.' I said, 'You've done what? Look, that's a driftway for the commoners' animals and its got to stay that way.' There was already a gate across the driftway. If you had animals, you had to let them through. There was a commoner lived over there and he said that was no problem. I was wild, I was. But in the end I said the committee, 'Look, I'm going to compromise. You say that cottage, that building is not on Forest land, but I say it is. But I'll compromise. You give us that piece of land that building is on, and you can come along there.' That's what was agreed. But they never did anything. They put a gate across the top of the driftway and this person used this piece of Forest land for car parking.

That driftway, there's no doubt whatsoever, was just sold for peanuts and there's number of the driftways like that have been lost, which is wrong. That driftway was put there for a purpose: for those commoners with common rights in the Sway area -- their animals - to drift down to the Forest - hence the word 'driftway' – it comes up all over the Forest.

Pilley Drift 1989: L-R: Len Mansbridge, George Kitcher and Sam Drodge

148

To be quite honest, to be a Verderer, if you're doing your job properly, it is time consuming. I don't mind telling you that: I had one or two disputes at home over that. I enjoyed it, but I always felt I was doing more good, the other side of the fence – on the Commoners' Defence. I was talking to Sir Dudley Forward one day. We were talking about being a member of the Commoners' Defence and all this, that and he said he didn't feel that a Verderer should be involved with the Forestry. He was a much more educated man than me – but we got on very well. The trouble with today – there's a different type of people in the Forest. My feeling is – is like commoners that are employed by the Forestry Commission, in my opinion, I don't feel that is the right thing for them to be elected as a Verderer. How can they attack their landlord – and their boss - on different occasions?

When Lord Manners retired and John Burry took on, it wasn't just the same. Up to a point I got on with John Burry, but it wasn't the same man. I can't explain why, but it wasn't the same. Then, one day John Burry and myself and Mrs Blick were at a meeting and John Burry asked me my age. And, I suppose I was a little bit hesitant, and I told him, 'I'm seventy-five.' And I knew – when I was elected, I knew, I was sort of over aged, you might say. But I never asked them to vote for me: I never did no canvassing. At the end of the term, I offered to stand again, but I knew I was too old.

Afterword

I began my Introduction by saying 'The history of the New Forest is the history of its commoners.' I now begin my Afterword by saying 'The future of commoning is the future of the New Forest.'

Daniel and Leonard Mansbridge were both born before the end of the First World War and, although there were 11 years between them, they shared a knowledge and understanding of a time that has long gone. Both of them saw the major changes that accelerated through the middle and late twentieth century: the change from the horse to motorised transport, the huge effects of the Second World War on the area, the advent of mass tourism and the increasing value placed on the area's natural environment by the country's population at large and environmentalists in particular.

With these developments came changes in the commoner's way of life from that of a productive agricultural and forestry community, enmeshed within the local rural and urban economy, to one seen as supporting an internationally important eco-system, and a landscape that attracts millions of tourists to the area each year. What they produce – whether it is ponies, cattle and pigs or milk, eggs and vegetables – is no longer as important as how they produce these goods. In a country which has limited and continually decreasing areas of precious wildlife and unspoiled open space, the New Forest landscape itself is the most precious good.

Today commoning is in some senses no longer viewed as an 'economic activity': commoners are providing 'a service' – and that is to supply animals to graze and browse the New Forest. Commoners are fully aware that commoning no longer *is* a profitable economy activity. At the present commoners can only survive if their activities are supported, either through government sponsored environmental schemes, or through money from their own pockets. Yet the landscape that commoning supports enjoys the highest status in ecological terms, as well as extraordinarily high house and land prices that can often only be paid by in-migrants to the area. As a result, the New Forest that commoning has sustained over the last decades and centuries, has become so attractive as a place to live and enjoy that it is in danger of excluding from its boundaries the very community that created it.

Len Mansbridge was rightly concerned about two major challenges facing the New Forest. The first was the reduction in the area available to the commoners and their animals as a result of encroachment, both on a large scale as with the fencing of the major roads, and a small one, as apparently minor infringements continually eat away at the open forest. He said, 'I wouldn't give an inch of the Forest away.'

His second concern was one of lack of understanding. The fact is that, although the commoners' stock – the grazing and browsing animals – are the most dominant feature of the New Forest landscape, the commoning community itself is almost invisible, and its views and deep understanding of the Forest are all too easily ignored. Len believed that local children should be taken to the Verderers' court, not just when it is empty and quiet, like a piece of history, but when it is in session, so that they can experience the reality of the way of life that sustains the New Forest. He understood that ignorance of, and lack of respect for, the commoning community would lead to the loss of the very cultural heritage that underpins the landscape, and without which it cannot be maintained.

Dan and Len are speaking to us today. We should listen.